INTROS, ENDINGS & TURNAROUNDS
FOR GUITAR

by Dale Turner

To access audio visit:
www.halleonard.com/mylibrary

Enter Code
1356-1523-8549-2760

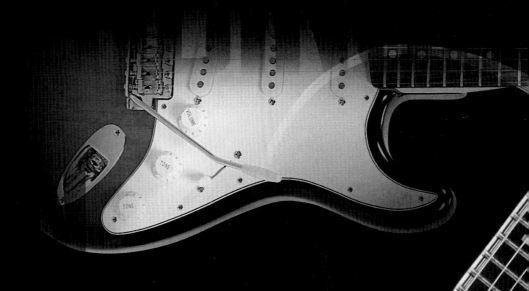

PLAYBACK+
Speed • Pitch • Balance • Loop

ISBN 978-0-634-02124-4

HAL•LEONARD®
CORPORATION
77 W. BLUEMOUND RD. P.O. BOX 13819 MILWAUKEE, WI 53213

Copyright © 2001 by HAL LEONARD CORPORATION
International Copyright Secured   All Rights Reserved

No part of this publication may be reproduced in any form
or by any means without the prior written permission
of the Publisher

Visit Hal Leonard Online at
www.halleonard.com

T004O624

Contents

About the Author

Dale Turner has authored numerous guitar instructional books for Hal Leonard Corporation and Cherry Lane Music, and transcribed dozens of note-for-note album folios for most of the nation's major publishers. He is currently the West Coast Editor of *GuitarOne* magazine, where he contributes everything from interview features and instructional pieces to performance notes and song transcriptions. Dale's written work has also appeared in *Guitar World, Guitar (For the Practicing Musician), Guitar School, Maximum Guitar, Guitar Techniques* (a UK publication), and *Guitar Player* magazines.

A member of David Pritchard's Acoustic Guitar Quartet (and featured on Pritchard's CD on Zebra Acoustic, *Unassigned Territory*), Dale has also performed with an array of renowned players—including Billy Cobham (Mahavishnu Orchestra/Miles Davis), Larry Klein (Joni Mitchell/Shawn Colvin), Eric "Bobo" Correa (Cypress Hill), and Josh Levy (Big Bad Voodoo Daddy), among others. He uses D'Addario strings and picks exclusively, and has featured the Line 6 POD Pro on numerous recordings.

In 1991, Mr. Turner received his Bachelor's degree in Studio Guitar Performance from the University of Southern California where he later went on to teach as a part-time pop/rock guitar instructor/lecturer (1993-95). Currently, he is a part-time instructor at Musicians Institute.

For more information, please visit Dale Turner at his own site on the worldwide web *(www.intimateaudio.com).*

Introduction

Have you ever been on the bandstand when somebody called out a blues, country, or jazz standard, and you weren't armed with a pre-established way to introduce the tune? The resulting "dead air" in front of an eager audience (while your band members argued over what to play) may have been enough to put you into cardiac arrest!

Do you have a sufficient vocabulary of tasty licks to "fill in the holes" left behind a vocalist's phrases at the end of a basic blues—the last four bars of the 12-bar form, referred to as a "turnaround?" If not, your days as a guitarist may be numbered. Can you navigate your way through the last string of changes in a 32-bar jazz standard?

Finally, do you have the material to effectively bring a blues, country, or jazz tune to a close? Even if you just played the best solo of your life, if the tune ends up fizzling to a stop (because nobody took the initiative and coughed up a "proper" ending), you may end up leaving the stage frustrated, your tip jar a little less than full.

The purpose of this book is to provide you—the multi-faceted guitarist—with a flexible collection of intros, turnarounds, and endings for each of these genres. Though many of the following figures speak for themselves, all are fully annotated and contain everything from chord progression analysis and technique advice, to tips for the application of each passage (including song-specific scenarios, in the case of jazz) and ways to maximize their usage. Some readers may even bypass the written text altogether and just listen to the accompanying audio tracks, then flip to the appropriate page to pick off the transcription. The choice is yours. The bottom line: If you're in need of a solid collection of riffs and licks that'll make you sound like an established authority in virtually any section of your average blues, country, or jazz tune, you've come to the right place.

—Dale Turner

Tuning

Creating "V-I" Cadences

In many cases, the overall success of an intro, ending, or turnaround depends on how convincingly the passage "sets up" the return of the tonic chord, often referred to as the "I" chord (e.g., a Cmaj7 chord in the key of C, or Cm in the key of C minor). By far, the most effective means of anticipating the return of the "I" chord is to precede it with the "V" chord (e.g., a G7 chord in the key of C). In blues, country, and jazz, this chord change is referred to as a "V-I" cadence (or "V-i," if cadencing to a minor key). In classical music theory terms, the "V-I" change is referred to as an *authentic cadence*. Given that the following intro, turnaround, and ending examples are written in a variety of keys, this table of "V-I" cadences may help you gain a deeper understanding of how these figures function—particularly if you plan on transposing them to other keys (once you've mastered them in their original keys).

Table of "V-I" (and "V-i") Cadences

"V7" (Dominant)	"Imaj7" (Major Tonic)	"im7" (Minor Tonic)	"I7" (Dominant Tonic)
G7 (G-B-D-F)	Cmaj7 (C-E-G-B)	Cm7 (C-E♭-G-B♭)	C7 (C-E-G-B♭)
D7 (D-F♯-A-C)	Gmaj7 (G-B-D-F♯)	Gm7 (G-B♭-D-F)	G7 (G-B-D-F)
A7 (A-C♯-E-G)	Dmaj7 (D-F♯-A-C♯)	Fm7 (F-A♭-C-E♭)	F7 (F-A-C-E♭)
E7 (E-G♯-B-D)	Amaj7 (A-C♯-E-G♯)	Am7 (A-C-E-G)	A7 (A-C♯-E-G)
B7 (B-D♯-F♯-A)	Emaj7 (E-G♯-B-D♯)	Em7 (E-G-B-D)	E7 (E-G♯-B-D)
F♯7 (F♯-A♯-C♯-E)	Bmaj7 (B-D♯-F♯-A♯)	Bm7 (B-D-F♯-A)	B7 (B-D♯-F♯-A)
C♯7 (C♯-E♯-G♯-B)	F♯maj7 (F♯-A♯-C♯-E♯)	F♯m7 (F♯-A-C♯-E)	F♯7 (F♯-A♯-C♯-E)
G♯7 (G♯-B♯-D♯-F♯)	C♯maj7 (C♯-E♯-G♯-B♯)	C♯m7 (C♯-E-G♯-B)	C♯7 (C♯-E♯-G♯-B)
C7 (C-E-G-B♭)	Fmaj7 (F-A-C-E)	Fm7 (F-A♭-C-E♭)	F7 (F-A-C-E♭)
F7 (F-A-C-E♭)	Bbmaj7 (B♭-D-F-A)	B♭m7 (B♭-D♭-F-A♭)	B♭7 (B♭-D-F-A♭)
B♭7 (B♭-D-F-A♭)	Ebmaj7 (E♭-G-B♭-D)	E♭m7 (E♭-G♭-B♭-D♭)	E♭7 (E♭-G-B♭-D♭)
E♭7 (E♭-G-B♭-D♭)	Abmaj7 (A♭-C-E♭-G)	A♭m7 (A♭-C♭-E♭-G♭)	A♭7 (A♭-C-E♭-G♭)
A♭7 (A♭-C-E♭-G♭)	Dbmaj7 (D♭-F-A♭-C)	D♭m7 (D♭-F♭-A♭-C♭)	D♭7 (D♭-F-A♭-C♭)
D♭7 (D♭-F-A♭-C♭)	Gbmaj7 (G♭-B♭-D♭-F)	G♭m7 (G♭-B♭♭-D♭-F♭)	G♭7 (G♭-B♭-D♭-F)

CHAPTER ONE

Essential Introductions

In this chapter, we will examine several familiar intros that can be used to introduce tunes in the blues, country, and jazz genres. Whether you want to launch an instrumental jam or open up a vocal tune, you'll find something that's appropriate for your unique musical scenario in this section.

Introductions often contain little nuggets of melody that are so familiar—intro clichés, if you will—that merely stating them will signal to an audience that something big is about to be introduced. For instance, how many times have you heard a figure such as this one kick off an event?

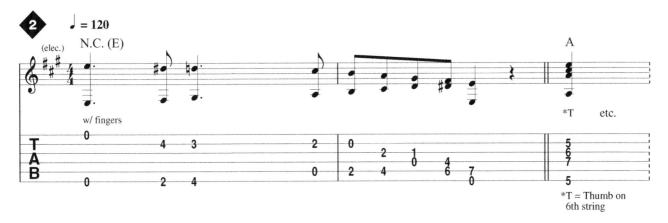

Needless to say, the power of clichés is undeniable. And in blues, country, and *especially* jazz, they are frequently exploited. As you digest the intros shown throughout this chapter, keep a look out for the recurring phrases that pop up in each style—like the subtle chromatic motion in various blues examples, scalar passages within a country riff, and cliché melodies buried deep within a chord-melody jazz passage.

Blues

A host of often-requested blues tunes—from "The Sky is Crying" to "Red House"—would fall flat on an audience's ears if they weren't "set up" with an appropriate intro. The guitar plays a pivotal role in launching your average blues number. So unless you're content with regurgitating the same generic intro lick in front of every tune (one word: boring!), you'd better get a few stock blues intros under your belt.

There are two primary approaches to introducing a basic blues: by performing licks/riffs in a manner that sets up the *tonic* chord (the "I" chord; the E chord in an E blues), or material that sets up the *sub-dominant* (the "IV" chord; the A chord in an E blues). In most cases, a simple four-bar figure will do the trick. In studying the following examples, keep your ears peeled for familiar phrases—instantly recognizable blues clichés that have stood the test of time. These types of intros are virtually failsafe, because you're hitting the audience with something they know right out of the gate. You'll also find them to be extremely flexible.

As a performance suggestion (when practicing with your band), play these intros unaccompanied for the first two bars (with only your drummer keeping time on his/her hi-hat), then bring in the full band on beat 2 of the third measure. You'll probably find this to be a fairly consistent (and easily recalled) formula.

Setting Up the "I" Chord

To easily convince an audience that they're about to be treated to a burning blues, start by reeling them in with a simple four-bar phrase that sets up the "I" chord by creating a "V-I" cadence in the intro's fourth bar. Typically, there are two ways to accomplish this: (1) Begin with a lead statement that outlines the tune's key center (the "I" chord), then briefly outlines other chords borrowed from the blues' structure (e.g., the "IV" chord) Follow this with a melodic statement that signifies the return to the tonic (the "I" chord). The entire passage is then punctuated with a "V" chord. (2) Perform a concise lead statement or accompaniment passage that outlines the chord sequence of a blues turnaround (the last four bars of a basic blues), often following a "V-IV-I-V" arrangement (in the key of E, B7-A7-E7-B7). The following illustration shows the chord changes inherent to a garden-variety 12-bar blues in E, with the aforementioned turnaround appearing on the bottom line:

	E7 (I)	A7 (IV)	E7 (I)	E7 (I)
	/ / / /	/ / / /	/ / / /	/ / / /
	A7 (IV)	A7 (IV)	E7 (I)	E7 (I)
	/ / / /	/ / / /	/ / / /	/ / / /
(turnaround:)	B7 (V)	A7 (IV)	E7 (I)	B7 (V)
	/ / / /	/ / / /	/ / / /	/ / / /

This first intro, tailored to fit any basic blues in the key of E, starts with a chromatically descending three-note sonority (bars 1-2), then unloads a burning E minor pentatonic (E-G-A-B-D) lick in bar 3 before puctuating the entire passage with a B7($\sharp$9) chord, setting up a return to the tonic (E7). As an added bonus, since this figure is comprised exclusively of fretted notes (i.e., no open strings), transposition becomes a piece of cake. Simply relocate the riff to another fretboard region, and you're off to the races!

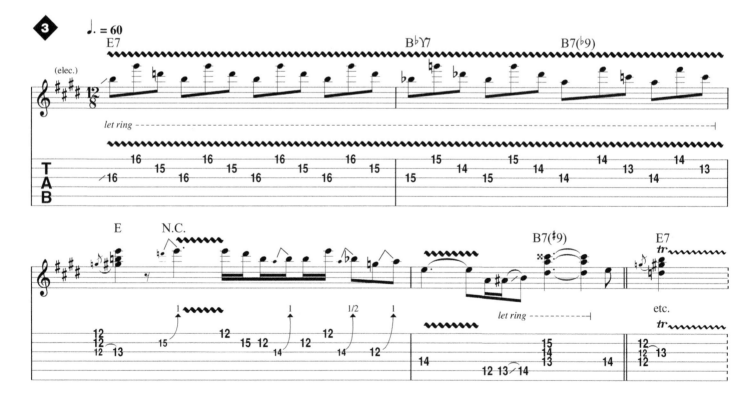

The next pair of intros borrows from a basic blues turnaround progression, setting up a "V-I" cadence in the keys of E and A, respectively. The first intro uses triads to outline a turnaround progression and is punctuated with an open-position blues fill and B7 chord. The second is driven by a basic boogie pattern, capped off with some familiar chromatic movement and an E9 shape.

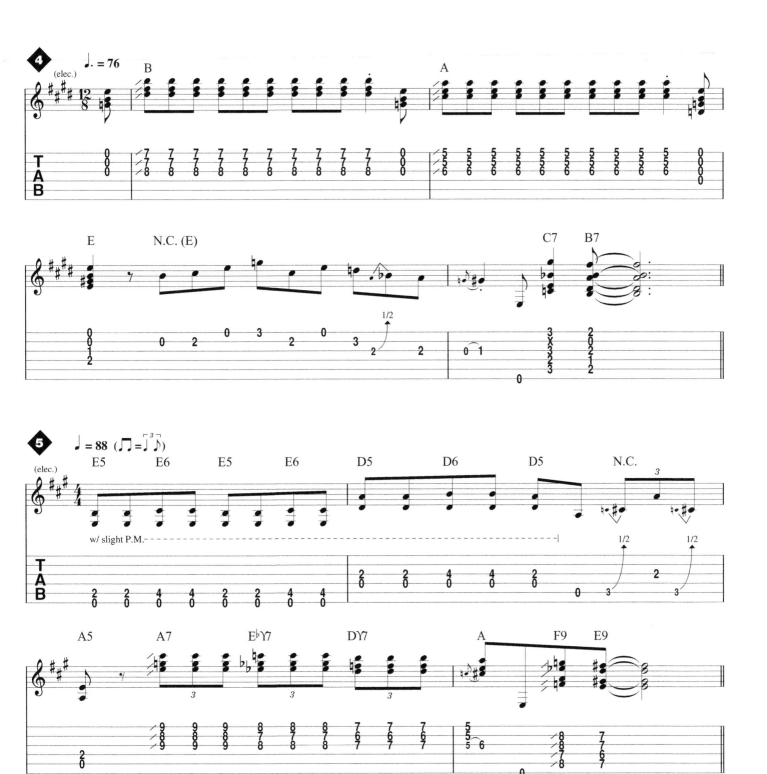

Here's another pair of intros derived from a typical turnaround progression, though they are a little quirkier. The first one is delivered with fingerstyle technique and superimposes different triad pairs over a fixed bass note (somewhat like Keith Richards' rhythm guitar work), culminating with a B7 chord. The second intro can be employed in any blues using a straight time feel (i.e., eighth notes that aren't performed with a triplet or "swing" feel). Though both figures are primarily chord-based, each of them packs maximum melodic punch due to the arrangement of pitches on the highest strings.

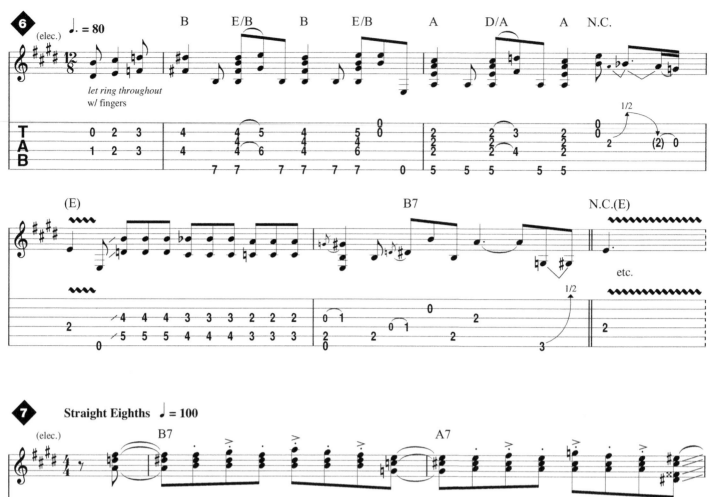

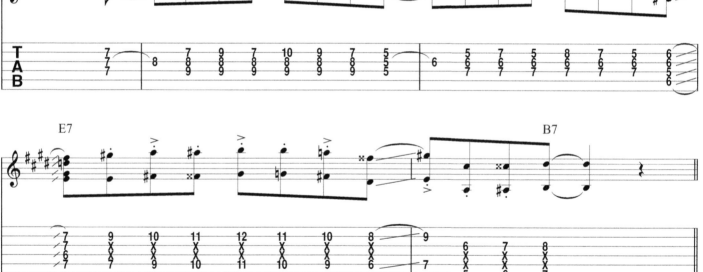

Of course, there are other ways to set up a blues without borrowing from turnarounds. Some blues tunes begin with the entire band burning right off the starting line, often hammering listeners with a progression that's a little more adventurous than the blues' typical "I-IV-V" structure—while a guitarist's lead soars over the top! In these types of intros, the interesting harmonic twist at the song's opening provides much of the musical drama. Here is a graphic depicting this kind of harmonic framework, written in the guitar-friendly key of E:

E7 (I)	D7 (♭VII)	A7 (IV)	B7 (V)
/ / / /	/ / / /	/ / / /	/ / / /

or

E7 (I)	B7 (V)	A7 (IV)	E7 (I) B7 (V)
/ / / /	/ / / /	/ / / /	/ / / /

So that you may hear these clever chord changes at work, this next intro features two guitars: a "lead" (Gtr. 1, panned hard left) and "rhythm" guitar (Gtr. 2, panned hard right). This will help clarify the chord changes—the E7-D7-A7-B7 progression—occurring behind the somewhat harmonically ambiguous E minor pentatonic lead line. In a "real life" scenario, the rhythm guitar chords in the following example would likely be played on a keyboard.

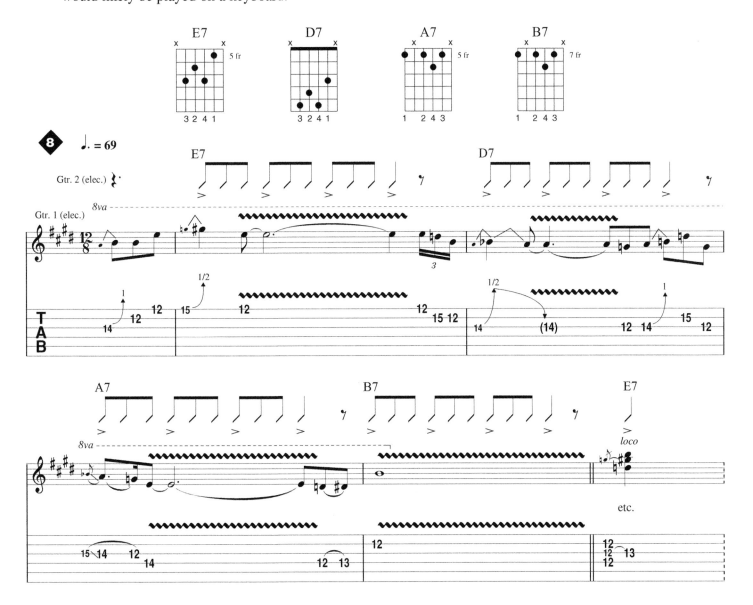

This next intro also begins with a full band. Here, the "lead" guitar part (Gtr. 1) is modeled after the types of bluesy intros you might hear an organist play. Notice that this intro's harmonic structure is still rooted in "I" (E), "IV" (A), and "V" (B) chords, but they're presented in a different order.

If you use this intro on the bandstand and you're playing as a trio (in which you're the only harmonic instrument), try to get your bass player to cop the boogie groove depicted in the Gtr. 2 part. If you want to go the extra mile and try to emulate the sound of a real Hammond B-3 organ, roll your guitar's tone all the way back (on a Strat or Tele, for instance) and employ a Leslie effect.

Setting Up the "IV" Chord

In some blues styles, an intro functions as a substitute—or "bypass"—of the first four bars of the blues form, prompting the band to enter on the "IV" chord and play out the song's remaining 12 bars before the song's "official" start point (e.g., where the vocalist enters). Typically, the instrument that plays the opening four bars (the true "intro") will improvise over the remaining eight bars of the form, thus creating the cumulative effect of a 12-bar intro.

The following intro, derived from a familiar blues/rock double-stop riff in C, can be used to kick off any supercharged blues performed in a straight-time feel. The instant you and your band hit the "IV" chord (F, in the omitted fifth bar), start improvising using tasty blues phrases rooted in C minor pentatonic (C-E♭-F-G-B♭).

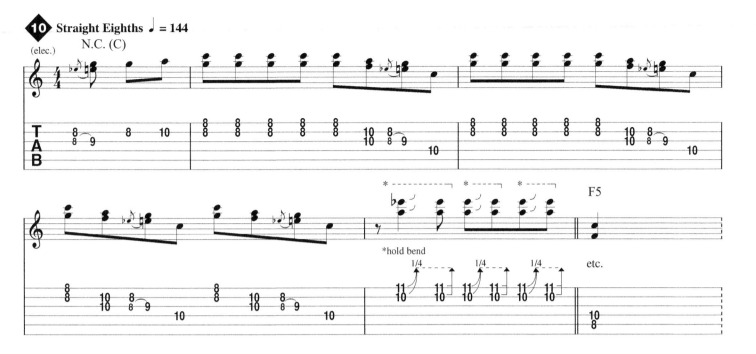

At some point during a blues gig, you may find yourself pulling out your acoustic guitar. In these instances, you may be expected to bust out your bottleneck and invoke the spirit of certain pioneering Delta blues guitarists.

The following acoustic slide intro, performed in the traditional slide tuning of Open-E (low to high: E-B-E-G♯-B-E), will fit the bill just fine. Again, this four-bar phrase is used to set up the "IV" chord (A) in an E blues. This means you'll need to get your slide chops together, since you'll have to improvise from the fifth bar onward.

Believe it or not, a fair amount of acoustic-based tunes from the Delta blues era actually begin with the "IV" chord and follow a form similar to this blues in E:

	A7(IV)	A7(IV)	E7(I)	E7(I)
	/ / / /	/ / / /	/ / / /	/ / / /
	A7(IV)	A7(IV)	E7(I)	E7(I)
	/ / / /	/ / / /	/ / / /	/ / / /
(turnaround:)	B7(V)	A7(IV)	E7(I)	B7(V)
	/ / / /	/ / / /	/ / / /	/ / / /

13

In these instances, a simple two-bar fingerstyle figure will suffice in setting the scene. Here's a pair of acoustic intros in E, both of which can be used to launch a blues with the "IV" chord (A).

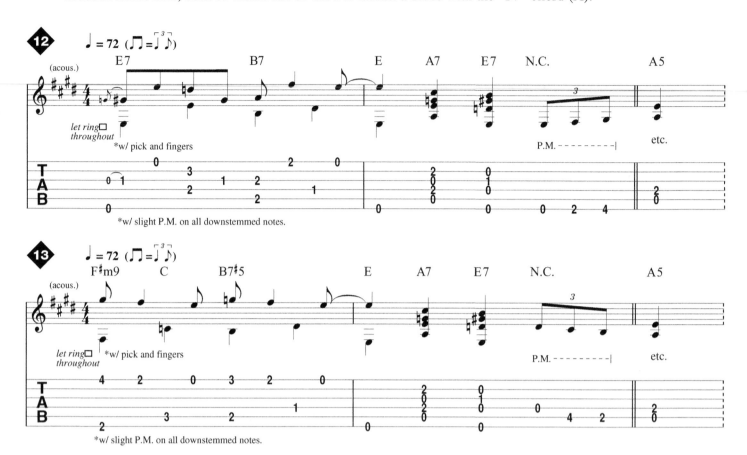

Country

There are countless ways to kick off a country tune, and a lot of that variety stems from the diversity of instruments used in an average ensemble. Most country bands feature both acoustic and electric guitarists, providing many options when it comes to launching a song. We'll start by focusing on the role of the acoustic guitar, since it's often the foundation of most country tunes. Keep in mind that all these intros, many of which are based on open-position chords, can be easily transposed to other keys by using a capo.

Hands down, the easiest way to start off a country song is to groove on an open-position "cowboy chord." Frequently, this chord will function as a "V" (e.g., "G"), setting up a cadence to the forthcoming tonic (e.g., "C"). In the following country intro, the cadence from the G to the C chord (in the omitted fifth bar) is made even more convincing with an ascending G-A-B-C scalar figure in the final bar. This act of walking straight up the scale from the root of the "V" chord to the root of the "I" chord is a key characteristic of classic country intros.

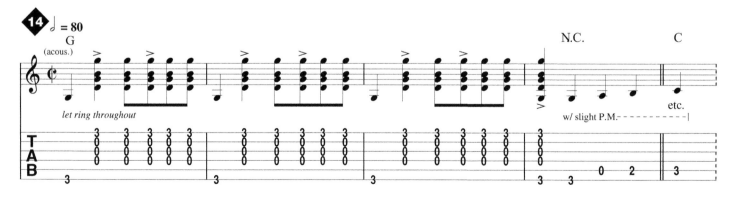

In country music, effective acoustic guitar intros can be created with a combination of alternating bass notes (usually the root and fifth) and routine strums. This approach, when played in the common country time signature of 3/4, features isolated bass notes on beat one, and strums on beats two and three. The result is an accompaniment passage that contains melodic movement (due to the shifting bass notes), clearly defined harmony (from the strummed chords), and an infectious groove (courtesy of the strumming rhythm).

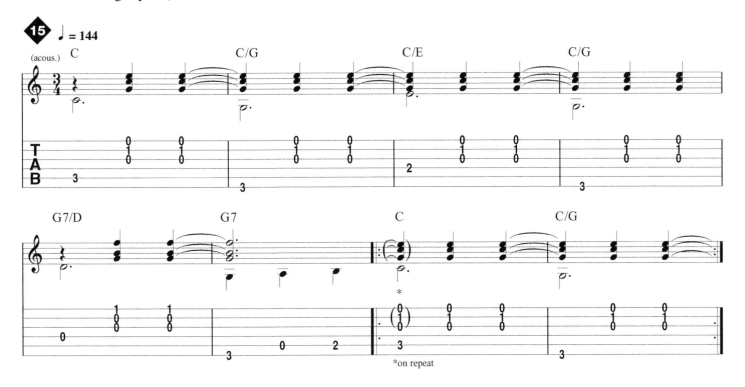

Here's another country intro in 3/4, this time using a pick-and-fingers technique. This hybrid picking approach makes it possible to project three separate parts: a melodic line on the highest strings (plucked with fingers), shifting bass notes on the lowest strings (played with the pick), and harmony filled in with the middle strings (picking the fourth string while the middle finger plucks the third string).

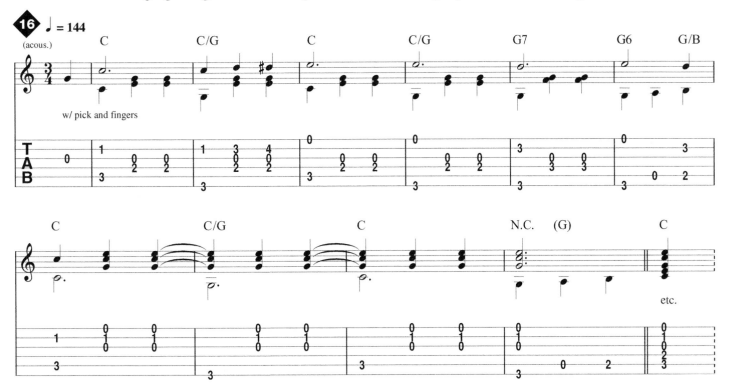

Like blues, country music is also ripe with cliché melodies that beg to be woven into the fabric of an instrumental intro. In the following trio of slow country introductions, a timeless "yodeler's" melody navigates its way through a series of shifting chords, performed fingerstyle. For maximum flexibility, this classic passage has been arranged in three different keys: C, D, and A.

If you're the Telecaster-wielding guitarist in your country outfit, your dazzling electric chops were likely honed on single-note phrases not unlike those in the following intro, suitable to kick off any uptempo

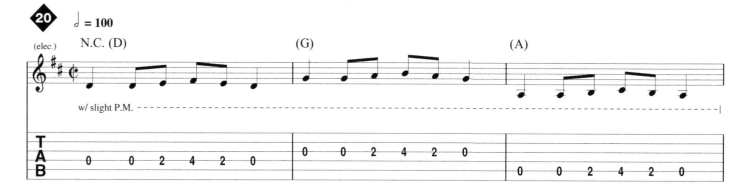

country classic in the key of D.

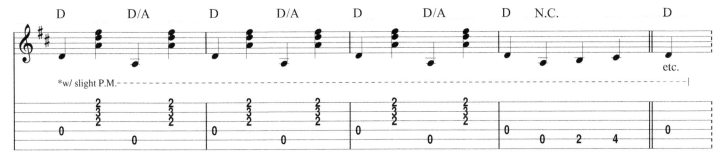

*w/ slight P.M.

*slight P.M. on ⑤ and ⑥

An electric guitarist's contribution to a country unit often entails adapting the types of lines best suited for another instrument—like a fiddle, banjo, or mandolin—to a Telecaster or Strat. This makes it possible for a smaller ensemble to tackle more tunes. By getting the following bluegrass-based banjo riff under your belt, not only will you enhance your pseudo-banjo chops, you'll also be armed with a show-stealing intro, worthy of any speedy country cut in the key of G.

This next intro cycles through a smattering of chords, including many from the dominant 7th family, using *Travis* picking technique. This style of picking, popularized by country guitar virtuoso Merle Travis, involves playing alternating bass notes with the thumb of your right hand (or thumb pick) while plucking melodic parts with your remaining right-hand fingers. Lightly rest the heel of your pick-hand near the bridge to slightly mute all the bass notes, while allowing the notes on the higher strings to ring freely.

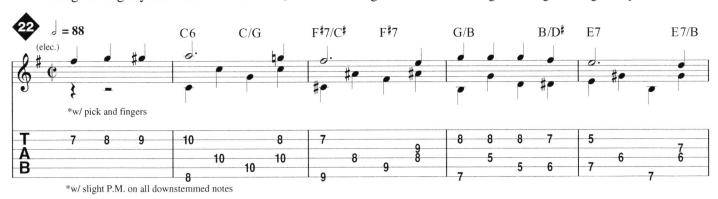

*w/ pick and fingers

*w/ slight P.M. on all downstemmed notes

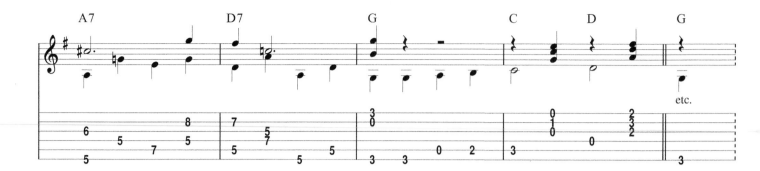

Travis picking can also be used to create nice signature riffs for country-rock tunes. These types of passages will often appear in the introduction and at various points throughout the song. In the following pair of intros, after a rock-inflected single-note riff on the lower strings, a Travis picking pattern takes over, setting up a country rocker in E. Keep in mind that each of the following Travis-picking riffs can also easily be substituted with any riff of your choosing. For this reason, you may regard the opening single-note phrases as the actual "generic" intro, as they're each adaptable to any situation.

This final country intro, which loosely implies an E chord, can open up any burning country-rock tune in the key of A. It can also be used to kick off an instrumental country jam in the key of E, if you treat the A chord in the omitted fifth bar as a "IV chord." (Refer to "Setting up the IV Chord" on p. 12)

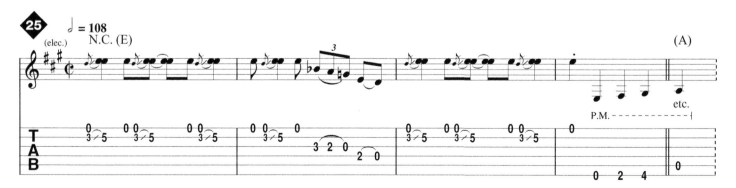

Jazz

If you're playing a jazz trio gig and your bassist pulls out the *Real Book,* you'll be expected to engage in an impromptu reading of a jazz standard—anything from a Gershwin classic to a Miles Davis tune. Since you're the only cat playing chords in the group, most intros will fall on your shoulders. What follows is a collection of jazz intros suitable for kicking off anything from a straight-ahead standard or bebop classic, to a Latin jazz number.

Jazz guitar intros generally fall into one of three categories: (1) chord vamps which essentially use one chord to set up the requisite "V-I" cadence; (2) a repeating two-bar cycle of generic changes (based on "Rhythm Changes," or a tune's closing "ii-V" cycle, etc.); or (3) a basic chord-melody arrangement using generic changes and containing either a fragment of the tune's melody, or one of several intro clichés.

Vamping On One Chord

Intros created from rudimentary vamps on one chord are by far the most versatile, simply because of their generic makeup—that is, they contain no "song specific" chord changes or melody fragments; their primary goal is to set up a cadence to the song's opening chord.

In the following pair of intros, a "V-I" cadence is created by milking the "V" chord for all it's worth—stretching out the chord's duration through the use of infectious syncopations. This helps build anticipation for the tune's melody.

The first figure sets up a "V-I" cadence in B♭, and could be used to set up a standard like "There Is No Greater Love." The second example exploits the "V" chord (F/G), setting up a cadence to the "I" chord (Cmaj7) with a dominant ninth chord positioned one half step above (D♭9). Try using this one to kick off a tune like on "On Green Dolphin St."

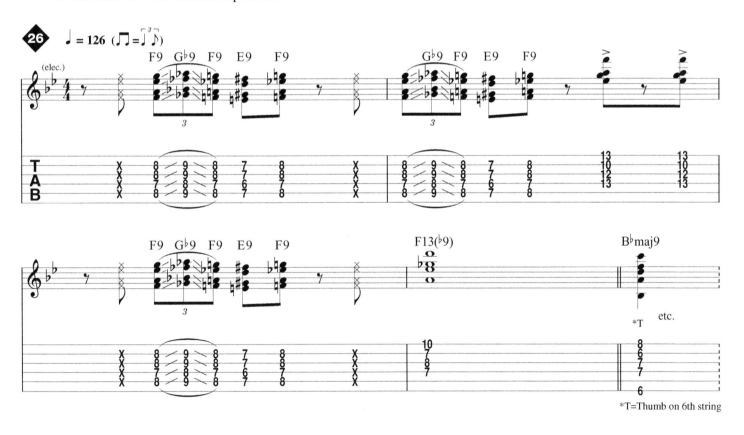

*T=Thumb on 6th string

19

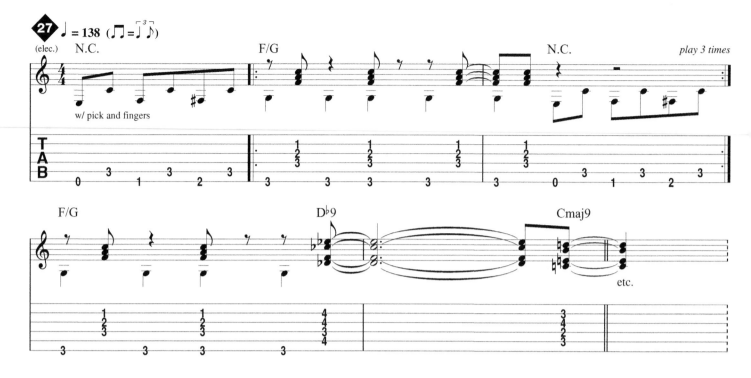

Here's another intro that sets up a "V-i" cadence, this time beginning with a few bars of vamping on the tune's tonic chord—alternating between Am (the "i" chord) and D/A—before the occurrence of the "V" chord, E7(♯9). This intro can easily be transposed to kick off any Dorian-based modal jazz tune—like "Impressions" (D Dorian), among others.

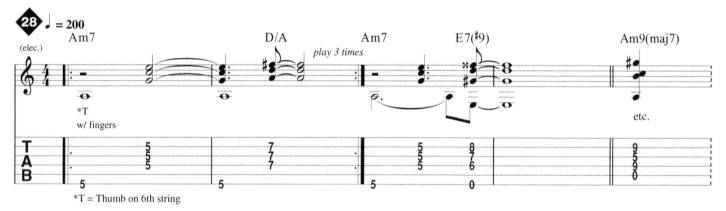

Chord Vamps Using Generic Changes

This next pair of chord vamps features derivatives of "Rhythm Changes"—specifically, "I-vi-ii-V" chord patterns fashioned from the Gershwin classic "I Got Rhythm" (and also employed in Sonny Rollins' "Oleo"). Because this chord sequence is so familiar, it can be used not only as an introduction to the aforementioned tunes, but also in front of any straight-ahead tune that starts on the "I" chord. Try using these to launch into any standard in B♭—from "Cherokee" or "My Romance" (in 4/4), to "Some Day My Prince Will Come," "Bluesette," or "Falling in Love with Love" (in 3/4).

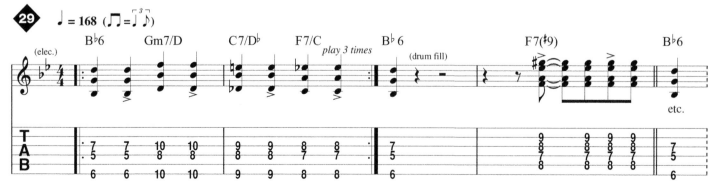

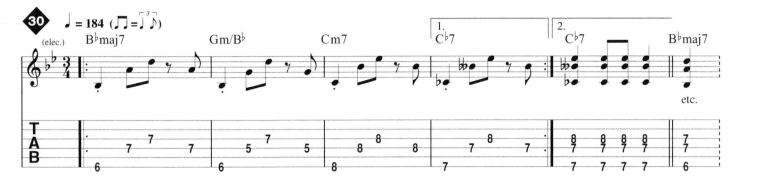

This intro also follows the B♭-based "I Got Rhythm" changes, but closes with a G7(♭9) chord (which acts as a "V" chord to Cm7). This makes it perfect for any tune in B♭ that begins with a "ii-V" (i.e., "Cm7-F7") change—like "Days and Nights Waiting." Or transpose the entire progression up a whole step to the key of C for use as an intro to "Satin Doll" (which opens with a Dm-G7 change).

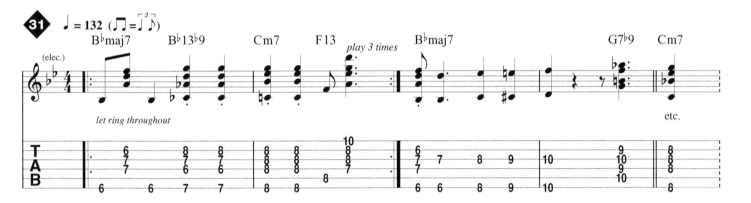

A jazz cut can also be set up with a string of chord changes that temporarily shy away from a tune's targeted tonality. In the following intro, a series of major seventh chords—A♭maj7, D♭maj7, and G♭maj7—create a dramatic link to a tune beginning with an Fmaj7 chord. Think of this almost as a "ii-V-I" sequence, comprised strictly of major seventh chords, cadencing to a key (G♭) one half step above that of your song (F). Try this one in front of a tune like "The Days of Wine and Roses."

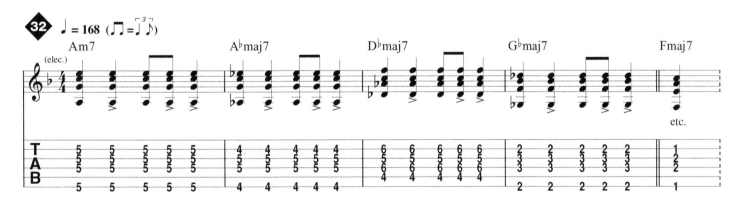

Chord Melody Arrangements Containing Intro Clichés

A step above strumming chords, "chord-melody" style playing combines the best of both worlds: harmony and melody in a singular guitar part. By simply stringing together chord inversions and playing fingerstyle, with a little practice, you'll be able to perform intros on par with jazz pianists.

This first chord-melody intro begins with a basic dominant seventh shape (C7), and uses passing chords and inversions to facilitate a familiar intro cliché on the second string. This two-bar phrase can be used to set up any tune that begins with a major seventh chord (in this case, Fmaj7)—like "Joy Spring," "Confirmation," or "Blues for Alice."

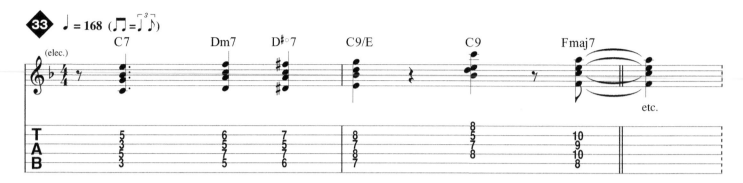

This next pair of intros is designed to kick off any standard in the key of G, but since neither involves open strings, they're both easily transposable. In each case, the final bar of the intro features an altered E7 chord. This is used to create a "V-i" cadence to Am7, making these intros perfect for setting up any jazz tune that begins with a "ii-V" (Am7-D7) change in G—like "I'll Remember April," "Ornithology," "How High the Moon," or "Autumn Leaves." (Note: the latter two standards contain pickup notes, therefore you may need to modify these intros.) The first intro contains the same cliché used in the previous example (in measures 7-8), while the latter introduces a different—though equally familiar—cliché in its final bars.

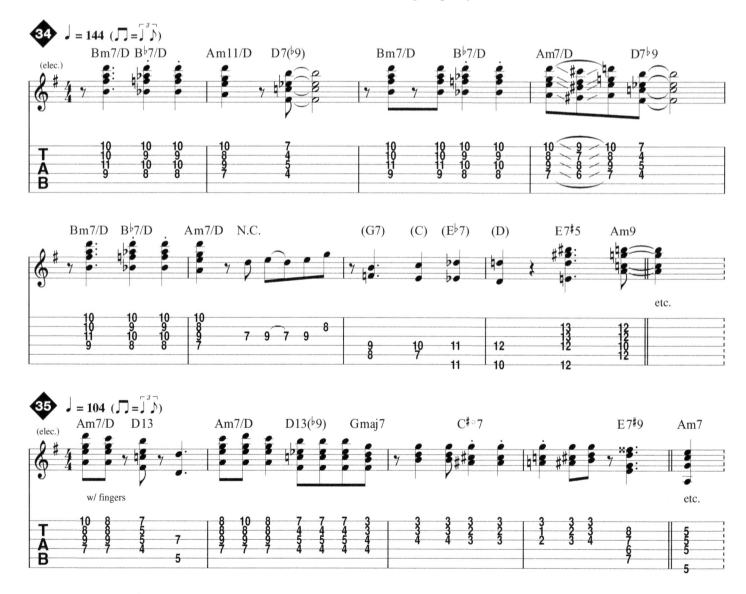

The next intro features a familiar melody, confined to each chord's highest string, stated over a "I-vi-ii-V" "Rhythm Changes" progression in F. There is also a walking bass line on the bottom pair of strings, supporting the chord and melody parts. The entire passage is punctuated with another cliché, again facilitated by passing chords and inversions.

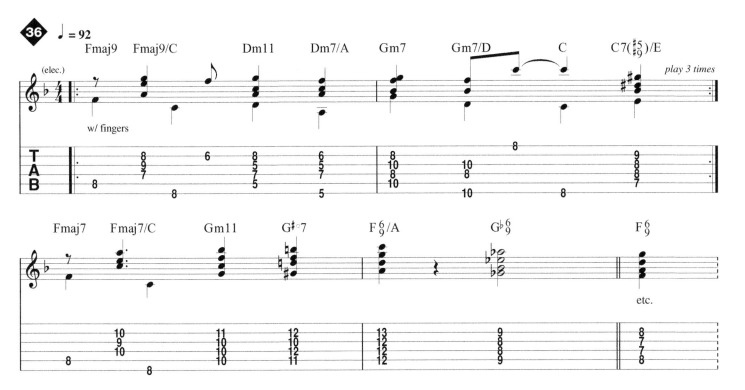

Latin Jazz Intros

Latin jazz tunes also play a prominent role in a jazzer's repertoire. It's a given that sometime you'll have to cop a guitar groove that properly sets up bossa novas like "Blue Bossa," or sambas like "One Note Samba." In addition, several swinging jazz standards are often performed with a Latin feel (i.e., in "cut time" and with a straight-time feel), or feature individual song sections driven by a Latin groove (e.g., "A Night in Tunisia"). In the interest of authenticity, all of the following Latin intro examples are performed on a nylon-string acoustic, played fingerstyle.

This first intro alternates between Cmaj7 and B♭maj7 chords, and can be used to set up any bossa nova or samba that falls in the key of C—like "Meditation," for example. Use your right-hand thumb to articulate each bass note on the fifth string, then pluck each three-note chord with your index, middle, and ring fingers. Note that this figure doesn't include the characteristic "V-I" cadence encountered in most intros; its distinct Latin groove and tonality create enough forward motion to set up the song.

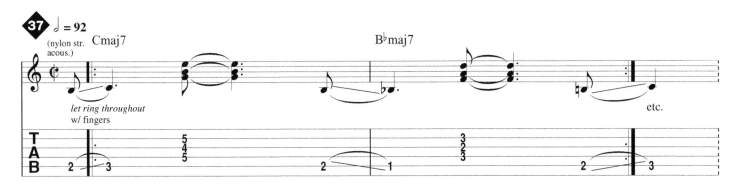

This next Latin jazz intro involves a chord pattern somewhat reminiscent of "Rhythm Changes," but its rhythmic treatment—syncopated double-stops on the middle strings, juxtaposed with fixed bass notes—creates a completely different vibe. Try using this intro to open up any Latin jazz tune in F—like "Girl from Ipanema" or "Summer Samba."

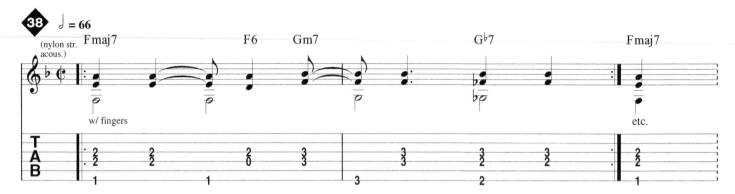

This next intro can be used to kick off any Latin jazz cut in a minor key. For our purposes, it appears in the key of Cm, making it a prime introduction for a track like "Blue Bossa," among others.

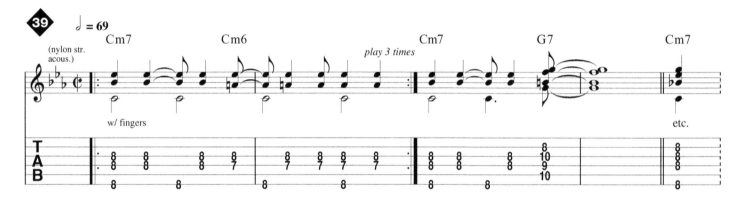

Here's another Latin intro that can be used for a tune in a minor key—in this case, D minor, making it suitable for familiar favorites like "How Insensitive," "Chega de Saudade" (a.k.a. "No More Blues"), or "One Note Samba." Notice that the bass notes assume a more active role, and the chord voicings are slightly more complex. It also contains a minor "ii-V" change (e.g., Em7♭5-A7♯5).

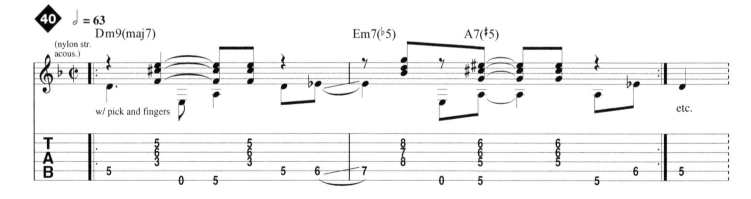

In Latin jazz groups, the pianist often sets up a tune with a familiar figure called the *montuna*. The following example is an adaptation of this piano part for nylon-string acoustic. This passage is characterized by a bass line that shifts between the root and fifth, and subtle, chromatic movement within chords (in this case, confined to the fourth string). Try using this famous intro to set up Latin jazz numbers in A minor—like "Black Orpheus" or "Recordame," for example.

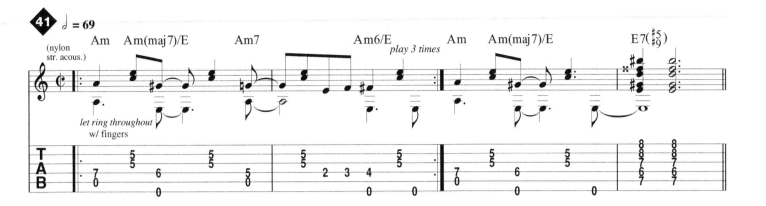

These last two Latin jazz intros are most effective when you're in need of something slightly quirky. The first cycles through derivatives of major seventh chords—moving in minor third increments—and can be used to set up virtually any tune in E♭, or transposed to a key of your choice. The latter intro also features chord shapes shifting in minor third increments, to maximum jarring effect, and is optimized for Latin numbers in B♭.

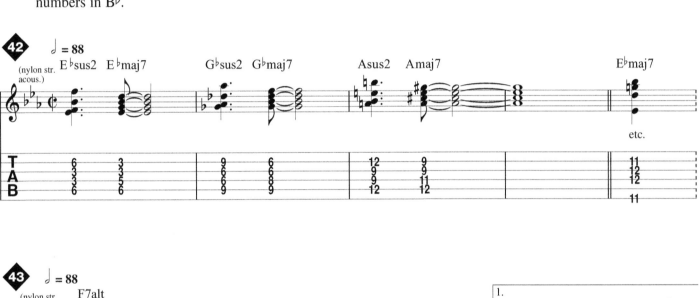

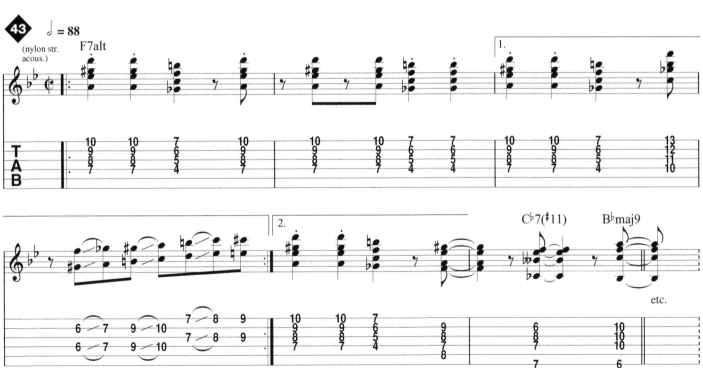

CHAPTER TWO

Essential Endings

How many times have you jammed on a blues, country, or jazz tune and not been able to bring it to an effective conclusion? With a few stock endings for each of these styles in your bag of licks, this problem will cease to exist. As always, keep your ears peeled for the ever-present cliché!

Blues

A blues ending, often referred to as a *blues tag,* is a phrase usually executed by the person playing the final solo in a blues number, signifying the end of the song.

As you play through the following E minor pentatonic (E-G-A-B-D) blues tag, which is ready-made for a blues in E, gradually slow down the tempo as you work your way toward the closing chord (E9). Remember: All eyes will be on you at this point—it's your job to cue the band. And the crowd goes wild!

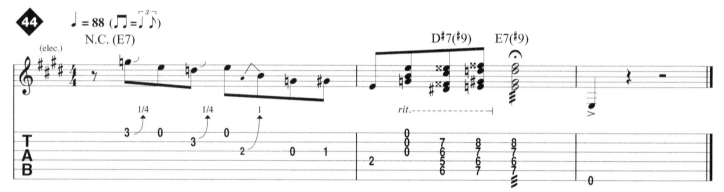

This next pair of tags can also be used to put the cap on a blues in E. Notice the different applications for double-stops in these two endings. The first inflects each note pair with a quarter-step bend, and like the previous example, ends dramatically with a tremolo-picked E7(♯9) chord. The latter uses hammer-ons in a double-stop context, closing with a common cliché played with pick-and-fingers technique.

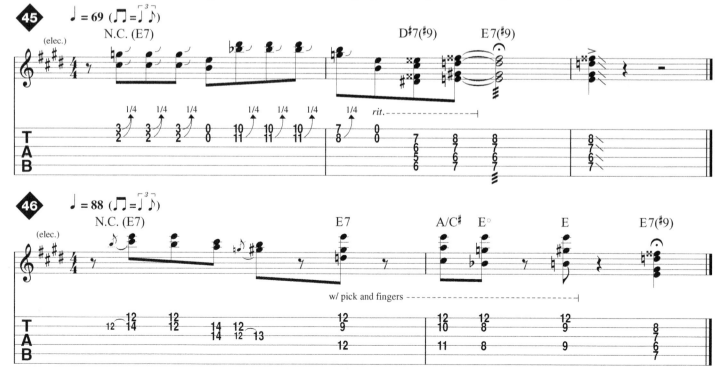

Here is a pair of classic endings for a blues in A, each performed in fifth position. The first tag applies a triplet-based bending pattern to each of the top three strings and ends with a chromatically-ascending dominant seventh (#9) shape, culminating with a tremolo-picked A7(#9) chord. The blues tag that follows uses a handful of descending double-stops to set up a climatic A9.

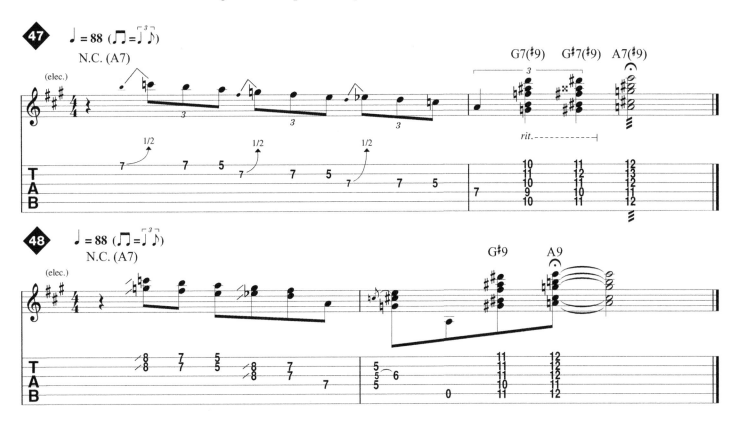

Blues endings can also be varied by using different arpeggiation techniques to double- and triple-stops, adding microtonal bends, and the like. Run your fingers through this next trio of blues tags, then try creating some of your own by mixing up the aforementioned techniques.

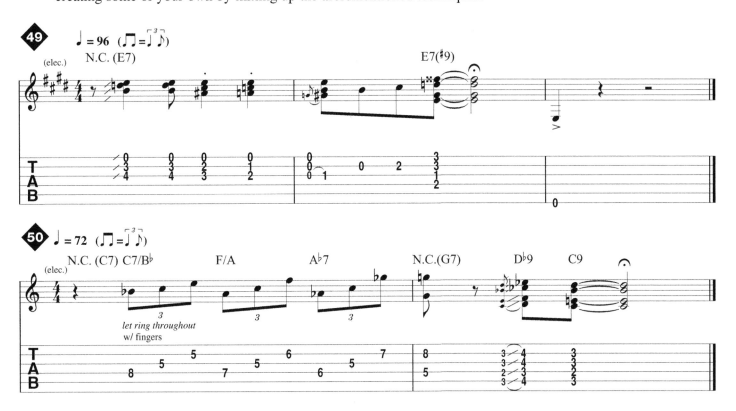

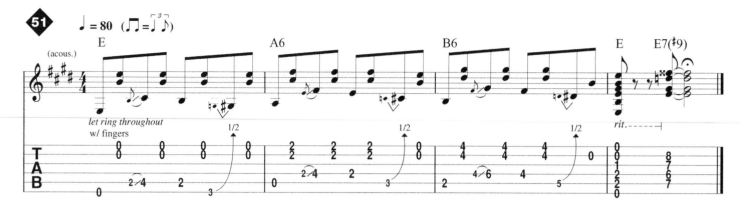

This final assortment of blues endings features more of a chord-based approach than in previous examples. But although single-note riffing is kept to a minimum in these chord phrases, there is still a good amount of melodic content. In each case, the smooth voice leading used to connect each chord puts the spotlight on the highest string, outlining familiar cliché endings as the chords are shifted around the fretboard. All of the following fit the bill for an E blues, except for the last tag, which is designed for a shuffle in A.

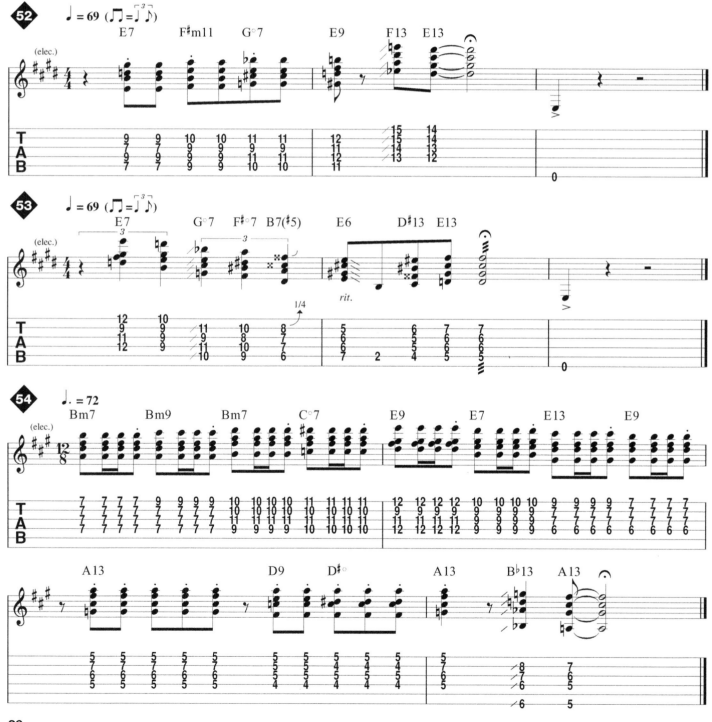

Country

Country tunes can be brought to a close in a number of ways: vamping on the song's last chord, tossing in an interesting harmonic twist, interjecting one of several classic bluegrass clichés (as commonly employed on fiddle, banjo, mandolin, etc.), or unleashing a barn-burning, country-fried double-stop lick. Whether you're playing an electric or acoustic instrument, you have a host of unique options when it comes to putting the cap on a country cut. Keep in mind that all of these endings, many of which are based on open-position chords, can easily be transposed to other keys with a capo.

This first country ending, written in the key of D, is a simple vamp on the song's closing chord (D). This chord is surrounded by an infectious D major pentatonic (D-E-F#-A-B) single-note riff ending on the G note (third fret, sixth string). This briefly implies the key center's "IV" chord (G). After three repetitions of this one-bar figure, an A7 chord sets up a "V-I" cadence to D, bringing the song to a convincing end.

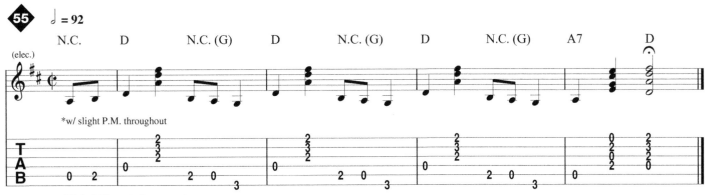

The next ending, designed for a country tune in A, inserts a dramatic harmonic shift by using chords outside the key—specifically C and F chords—prior to the requisite "V-I" change (e.g., E to A). Notice that the closing A chord gets an interesting treatment: the triad shape on the second fret is slid up to the 14th fret (one octave higher). This approach can be used with virtually any country tag that ends with an open-position chord.

Here's a pair of classic country endings, each of which borrows a familiar "fiddle" line from the bluegrass vocabulary, performed in the key of G on acoustic guitar.

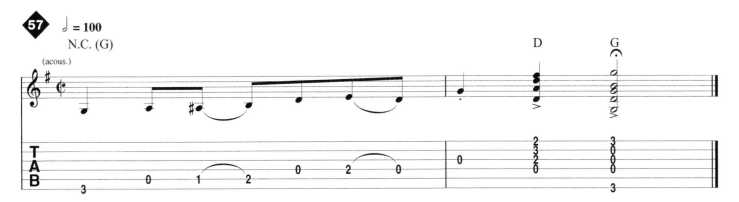

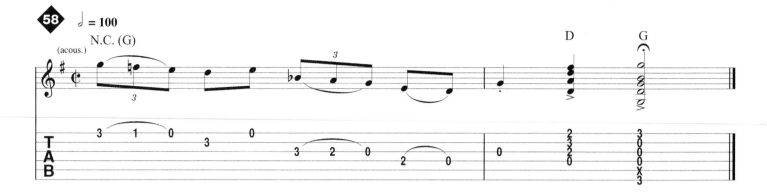

This next ending is a lengthy scalar passage in open position, primed for a country cut in the key of C. In this type of fancy ending, the entire band typically lays out (except for the drummer, who keeps time on his/her hi-hat) until the last bar, while the guitarist cranks out his/her fiddle-inspired lines. These types of endings can be performed at any tempo, from medium-fast to absolutely blazing.

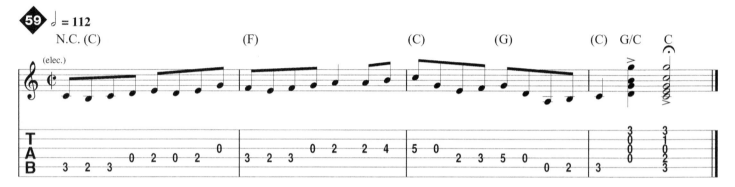

An electric guitarist often has the opportunity to wrap up a country tune with a quick double-stop lick. Like the previous example, this type of phrase may also be performed unaccompanied, with the band entering dramatically the instant you hit your lick's final note.

Given that this double-stop lick contains several bends, you'll need to pay careful attention to your intonation. For this reason, you'll need to use a guitar with a fixed "hard-tail" bridge (e.g., a non-tremolo equipped guitar like the Fender Telecaster). Nothing sounds worse than an out-of-tune bend in conjunction with a stationary note! Try this one at the end of any country tune in G.

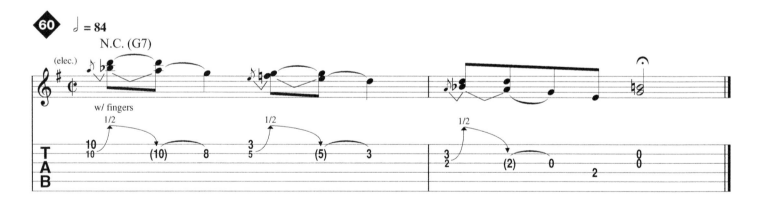

This last handful of country endings should provide you with a wealth of bluegrass-inspired clichés. Each occurs in the vicinity of open position (key of G), and is performed at a quick tempo, requiring good alternate-picking chops. For best results, dust off your metronome, use it to establish a comfortable practice tempo, and gradually work these endings up to the indicated speed.

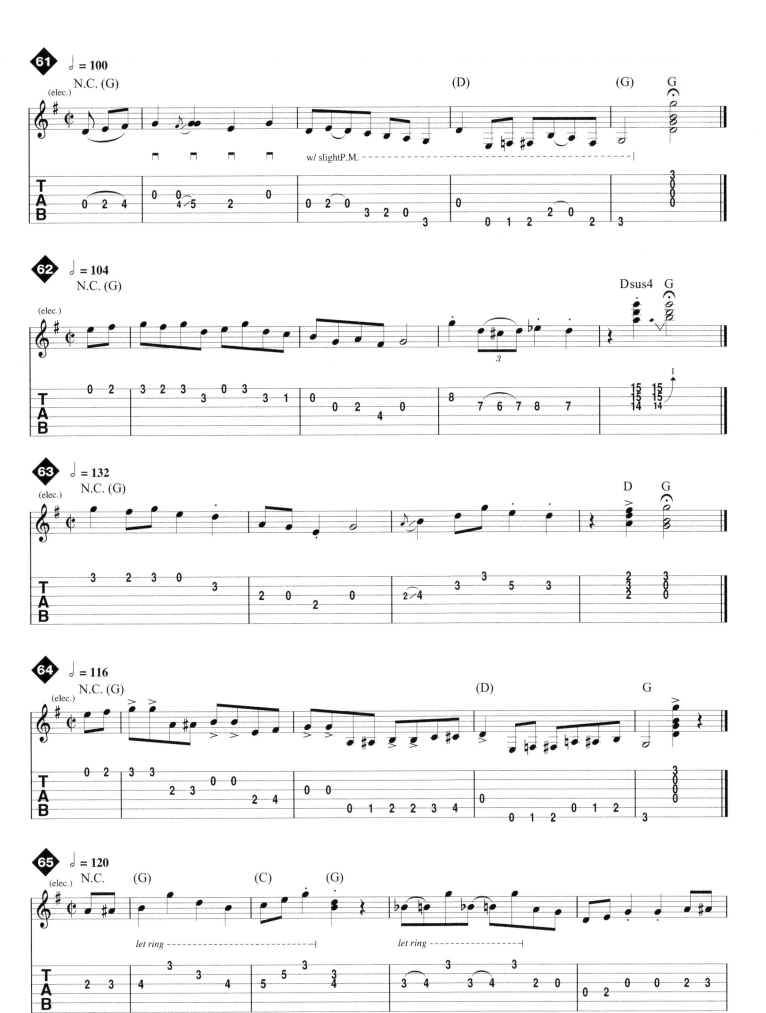

Jazz

Because of the variety of instruments featured in jazz ensembles, the vast number of common chord cycles, and the diversity in time signatures, tempos, and feels, you'll need to have a variety of endings under your belt if you want to feel comfortable playing in any jazz scenario. A short list of industry-standard endings would have to include: rubato endings, endings featuring clichés, endings derived from chord vamps, endings featuring cadenzas, and endings suitable for Latin jazz. You'll also need to know what to do when *another* instrument unleashes one of these types of endings. This is particularly important when a saxophonist or pianist launches into a cadenza. In this segment of the book, these five "jazz ending" categories will be explored in-depth.

Rubato Endings

Rubato endings (passages played free of rhythmic time constraints) are very common in jazz tunes—particularly in ballads and medium-tempo standards. In a typical "guitar trio" setting (guitar, bass, and drums), the only instrument that can accomplish this is the guitar. Therefore, you'll need to have woodshedded a few chord-based fingerstyle passages if you want to dazzle onlookers with your rubato endings.

This first pair of rubato endings explores major seventh chords, maneuvered around the fretboard in a way that naturally sets up the return to the tonic, Gmaj7. In both cases, the fingerstyle approach involves plucking the outermost chord tones simultaneously with the thumb and ring finger, then filling in the middle of the voicing with the index and middle fingers. The chord voicings used are virtually identical throughout, merely transposed to new tonal areas.

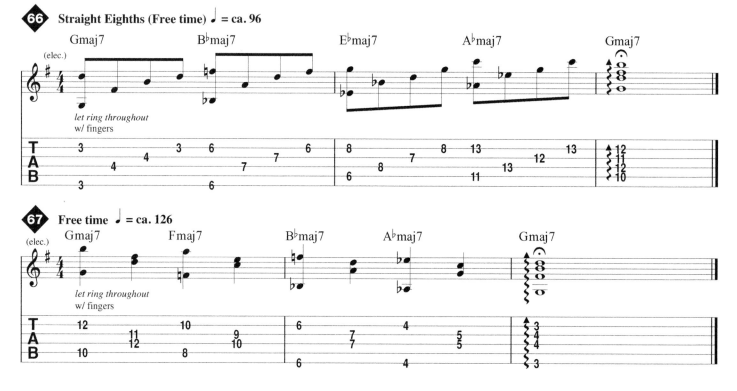

The next example can also punctuate a jazz standard in the key of G. Here, each chord is dictated by a chromatically descending bass line on the sixth string. When you reach the final Gmaj7 chord, while the chord is sustained, reach down to your guitar's volume knob and quickly oscillate it back and forth. This manual tremolo effect is common in jazz guitar endings.

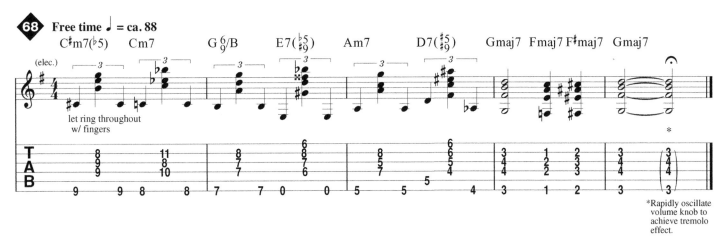

In the Jazz Turnarounds section of this book, we will see that the final bars of an average standard feature a "ii-V" cycle. When performed rubato, these types of cycles can also create effective endings. This next ending, designed to punctuate a tune in B♭, employs a common Dm7-G7-Cm7-F7 cycle, "jazzed up" with tritone substitution (replacing G7 and F7 with D♭13 and C♭13, respectively) to create a chromatically descending bass line along the sixth string.

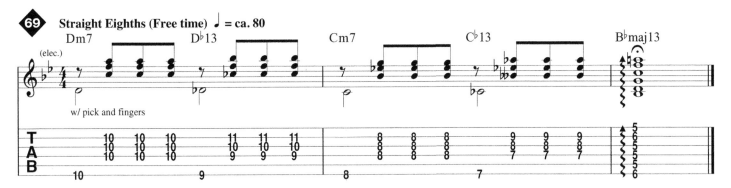

Endings Featuring Clichés

This jazz ending, written in the key of B♭, features an effective chord-melody passage up front, and is punctuated with a classic cliché in the final bars. It closes with a B♭6/9 chord, one of the most common "jazz ending" chords you're likely to come across.

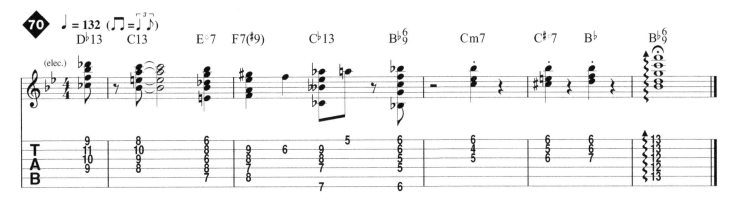

The next three examples feature cliché endings in their latter bars. The first, written in B♭, begins with a string of diminished chords, descending the fret-board in minor third intervals before arriving at an F7

chord and launching the requisite single-note phrase. The next ending can be used for any tune in the key of C, and uses chromatically descending minor seventh chords before its cliché melody is unleashed. The last ending takes a basic "ii-V" cycle (Cm7-F7) in B♭ and expands it by transposing it up a whole step (Dm7-G7). (Note: This approach can be used with almost any tune that ends with a generic "ii-V" chord change.) A final "ii-V" cycle (Cm7-F7) then sets up a cliché lick in B♭, played in double stops.

In fact, virtually any jazz ending can be punctuated with one of these types of clichés. As an exercise, transpose as many clichés as possible to the keys of C, F, and B♭ and try inserting them after the opening two bars of any of the jazz endings in this section.

Ending Vamps

A song's closing chord cycle can often be repeated to create a makeshift ending. This example repeats a stock Dm7-G7-Cm7-F7 chord change to set up an ending in B♭. Notice that the majority of chords performed throughout are reduced to two-note voicings, creating rhythmic and sonic space for intermittent melodic fills.

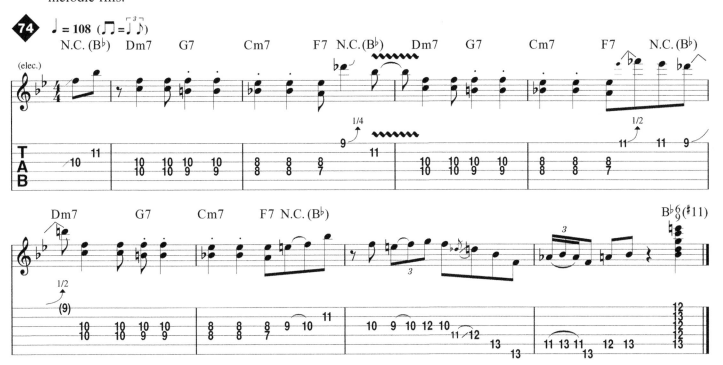

This next ending uses an approach similar to the previous passage, but it vamps on a D7-G7-C7-A7 progression before engaging in a "V-I" cadence in C. Incidentally, this passage features one of the most popular cliché endings under the sun. When it comes to creating convincing endings, phrases like these are invaluable.

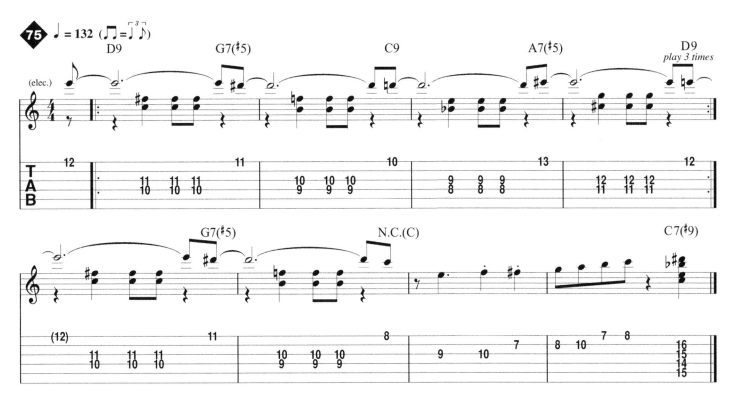

Using chord changes reminiscent of our familiar Dm7-G7-Cm7-F7 chord progression, this ending uses a healthy dose of dominant seventh chord derivatives (e.g., D7#5-Ab9-G7b5/#9-Db13) in its opening bars to create a vamp that sets up a cadence to Bbmaj9. The melodic content owes much to voice-leading—minimal motion between notes in each chord, which draws attention to the uppermost notes in each voicing.

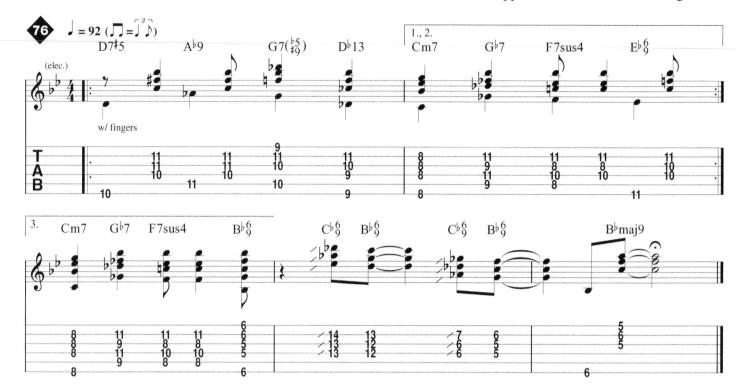

This last ending features a chord cycle driven by chromatic motion on the bass strings, punctuated with a "ii-V" change (Dm7-G7) in C. What is interesting about this ending is the fact that the "V" chord, G7(#5/#9), is strummed for an extended time before its cadence to Cmaj13. In a "real-life" situation, this portion of an ending would likely feature a soloist in an intense improvisation, cueing the band when it's time to end on the Cmaj13 chord.

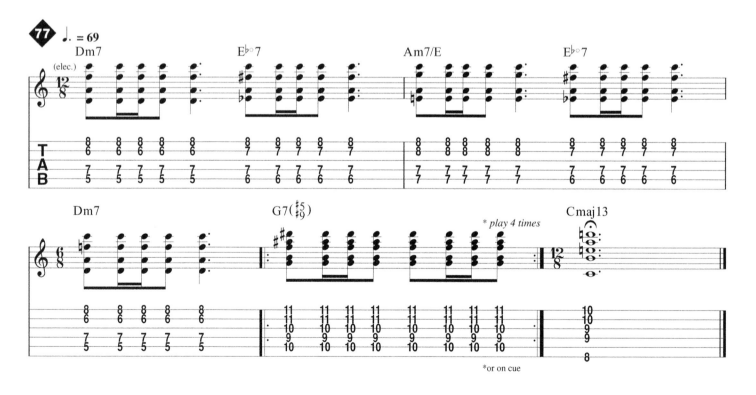

Endings Featuring Cadenzas

If your ensemble features a burning improviser, you'll want to provide an opportunity for him/her to shine in a *cadenza* at the end of a jazz tune. While an accompaniment instrument sustains a chord, the soloist will execute phrases in free time, splattering the proceedings with blazing runs and sequences.

In this next pair of endings, a sustained chord (in both cases, an altered dominant seventh chord) provides a backdrop for your saxophonist, trumpeter, or pianist to blow over. Often, when the soloist completes his/her cadenza, the tune will be punctuated with an arrangement of major seventh chords, climbing up chromatically from a whole step below the tonic, as in the first example. As an alternative, a cadenza can culminate with the cliché phrase depicted in the second example.

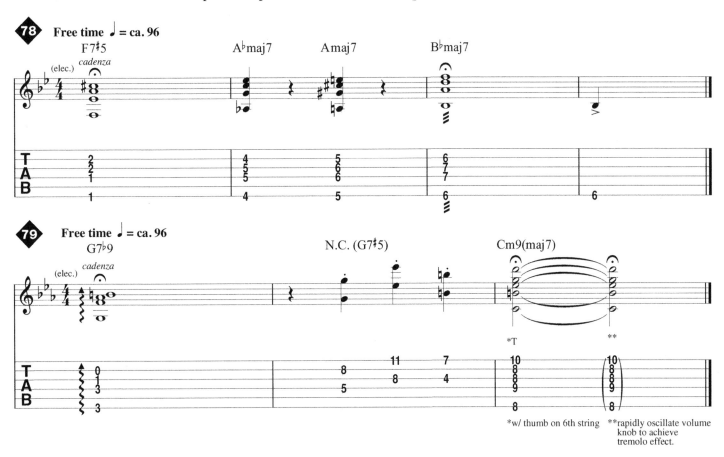

Of course, there will come a time when you'll get the opportunity to unleash a cadenza of your own. The next pair of jazz endings depicts two distinctly different types of cadenza approaches that could be applied to the key of B♭. The first begins with a rubato chord-melody solo, and climaxes with a quickly executed series of phrases over the tonic chord, B♭maj7.

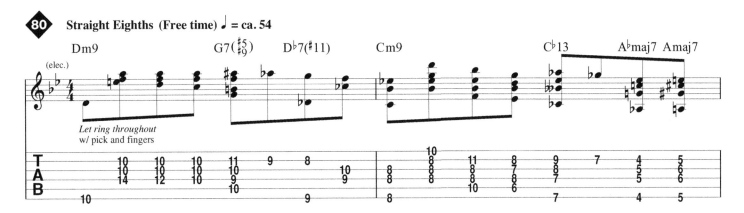

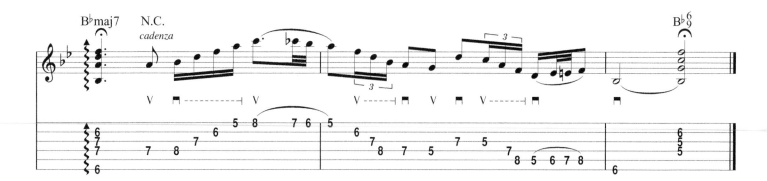

This next cadenza example features *harp harmonics*—a technique that can be used to create a cascading series of bell-like pitches that bleed together. The result is not unlike what occurs when you depress the sustain pedal on a piano, or run your fingers over the strings of a harp. To execute this technique, begin by laying your fret hand flat across the third fret. Next, position your right-hand index finger over the 15th fret (exactly 12 frets higher) and allow your fingertip to lightly touch the string. To create the harmonic, simply pluck the string with your right-hand thumb.

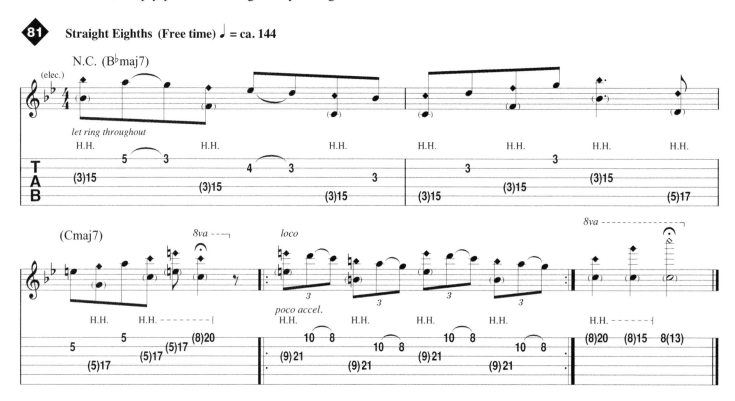

This last cadenza can be used over any dark, brooding standard in the key of A minor—like "What Are You Doing the Rest of Your Life" or "Black Orpheus," for example. The passage involves an ascending array of intervals (thirds, fourths, and fifths) from A minor pentatonic (A-C-D-E-G), with an occasional deviation into E♭, arrived at using tritone substitution.

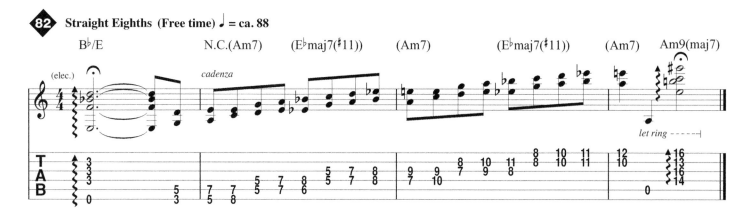

Latin Jazz Endings

Many of the two-chord vamps in the "Latin Jazz Intros" portion of this book (p. 23) can also be used as outro vamps. However, in Latin numbers in a minor key, there are certain chord cycles that are commonly employed. This final pair of endings can be used to wrap up any Latin jazz tune that falls in the key of D minor. Each involves subtle chromaticism (note the chromatically descending bass line in the first example) and slightly pushes the tune's harmonic boundaries (note the use of both G major and G minor chords in the latter example). The first ending culminates with a Dm9(maj7), while the latter ends on a more positive note, cadencing to Dmaj13.

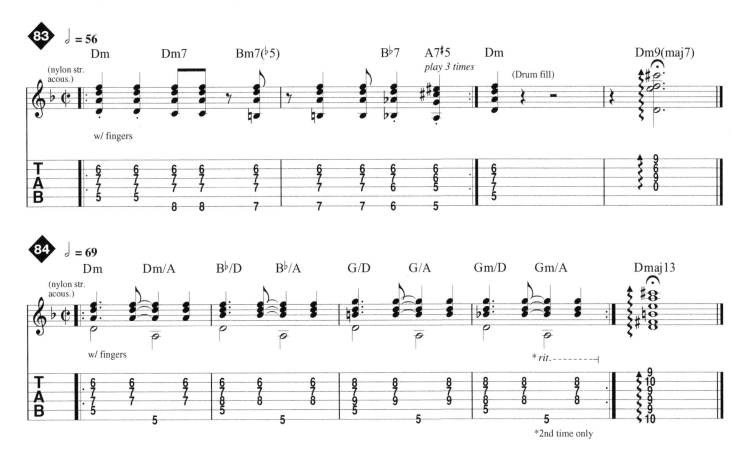

CHAPTER THREE

Essential Turnarounds

Highly improvisatory music forms like blues and jazz employ a wealth of familiar phrases and chord changes which signify the end of a song's form, indicating that the entire chord cycle will repeat and the vocalist may take another verse, or the soloist may take another chorus. Over the next few pages, we will explore several familiar licks and accompaniment passages within these two styles. Once you're able to play them, transpose them to at least all the common blues (e.g., E, A, and G) and jazz (e.g., F, G, B♭, E♭, and A♭) keys.

Blues Turnarounds

A blues turnaround is a lick that fills in at the end of the 12-bar blues form, prompting the band to "turn around" and return to the beginning of the form. On average, these types of licks feature about 1-1/2 measures of leadwork, punctuated by the key's "V" chord. (Note: they may also be plugged into the final two bars of virtually any blues intro.)

In this first blues turnaround, sixths are arpeggiated with a combination of pick and fingers in measure 1, while an E9 chord—the "V" chord in an A blues—puts the cap on it in measure 2. Notice that the E9 is preceded from one half step above by an F9 chord. This half-step movement into the "V" chord—approached from above or below—is a common characteristic of most blues turnarounds.

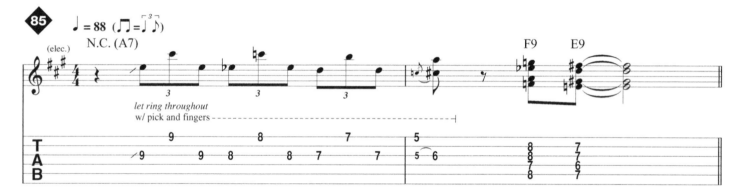

You can get maximum mileage out of a blues turnaround by simply varying the manner in which you perform its core materials. Each of the following three turnarounds begins with a chromatically descending dyad (two-note sonority) on the second and third strings, played in conjunction with the open E string. Try these out in the final bars of any E blues.

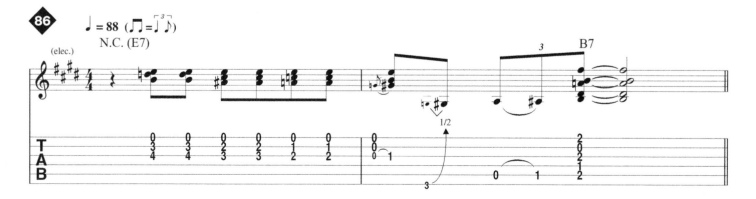

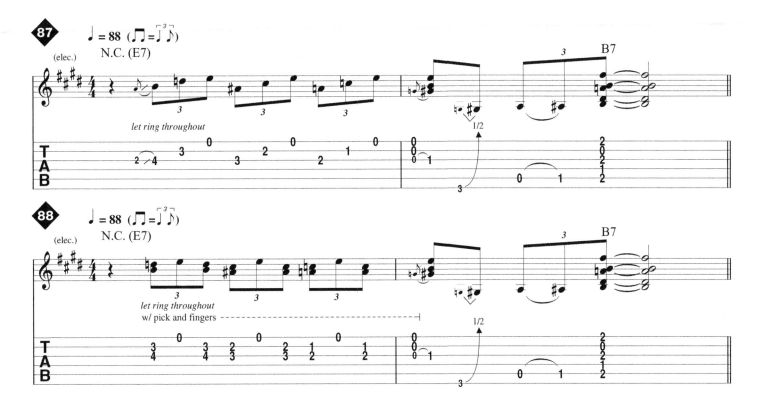

As the previous three examples demonstrated, by simply varying your arpeggiation technique, you can create a completely new turnaround. See if you notice this concept at work in the next pair of turnarounds, each of which is tailor-made for a blues in A.

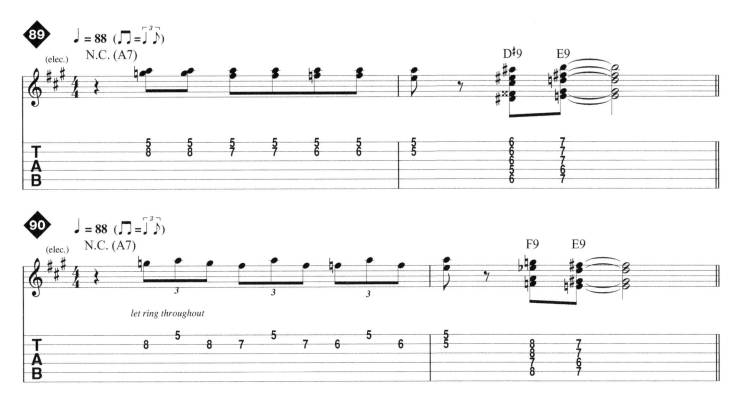

As you've probably noticed by now, chromaticism plays a key role in creating killer turnarounds. Up to this point, chromaticism has been used in a strictly *descending* manner. In this next pair of turnarounds, the shape used at each figure's outset is essentially the same. But notice how chromaticism is employed in the latter example—*ascending* the second string—creating extra dramatic tension before culminating with an E7 chord. Once you get both of these figures under your fingers, try experimenting with them by using different arpeggiation techniques to maximize their flexibility.

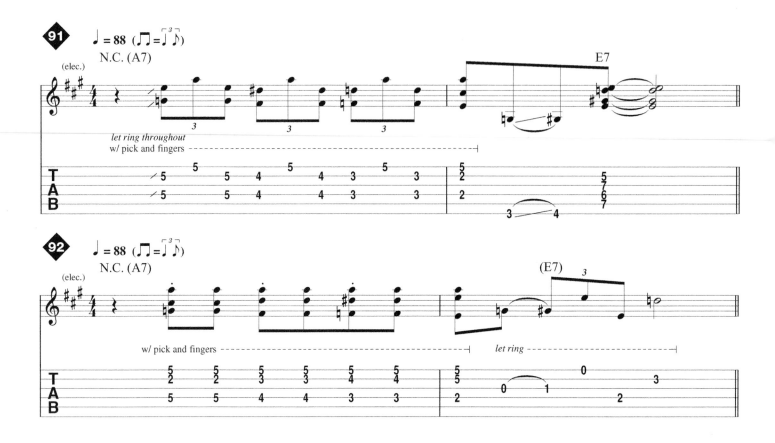

Of course, in a turnaround comprised strictly of single notes, techniques like arpeggiation can no longer be used, so variations are limited. But since your fret-hand no longer needs to grapple with two- and three-note sonorities, you can tap into a wealth of phrasing devices that are otherwise unavailable—lead guitar techniques like hammer-ons, pull-offs, string bending, and vibrato.

In this final pair of blues turnarounds, single-note phrases are used to set up the "V" chord. The first of these two turnarounds, designed for use in an A blues, uses ascending chromaticism along the third string. The second example, fashioned for a slow blues in G, uses each of the aforementioned "lead guitar" phrasing devices.

Jazz

In jazz, a turnaround serves much the same purpose as in the blues: to mark the end of a song's form and set up the return to the top of the tune for another statement of melody. However, because of the harmonic sophistication of jazz, there are many more "turnaround" possibilities than in blues. A jazz guitarist should have not only a variety of chord voicings and comping patterns under his/her belt to navigate a tune's turnaround, but also single-note chops and improvisational skill to "blow" through such changes. In this section of the book, a variety of single-note solos will be presented along with chord changes and accompaniment patterns commonly employed in jazz turnarounds, performed by Gtrs. 1 (panned hard left) and 2 (hard right), respectively.

I-VI-ii-V Progression

One of the several common chord cycles used to close out a jazz standard resembles the "Rhythm Changes" in the jazz section of this book's "Essential Introductions" chapter. In the following turnaround, a "I-VI-ii-V" progression is outlined using basic seventh chords (Gtr. 2), while a walking bass line connects each voicing. Notice that this bass line makes use of "upper neighbor" tones, anticipating each chord with a note one half step above (e.g., an A♭ leading into G7). This is a quick and painless way to squeeze effective bass lines out of garden-variety, root-position seventh chords. Meanwhile, the single-note lead line of Gtr. 1 makes heavy use of chord tones, with occasional alterations—like the ♯11 (the E played over B♭maj7), ♯5 (the D♯ over G7; the C♯ over F7), and ♭9 (the G♭ over F7).

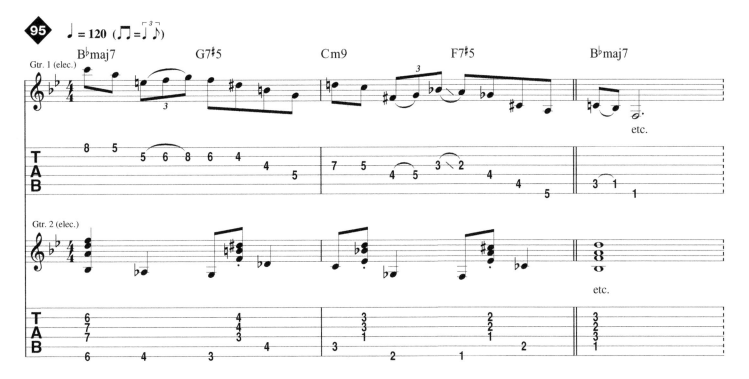

ii-V Cycles

One of the most common chord patterns used at the end of a jazz standard's form involves using the key center's *mediant* chord (the "iii7" chord) as a "jumping off" point for a descending "ii-V" cycle. In the key of B♭, this type of turnaround will feature a pair of back-to-back "ii-V" changes (Dm7-G7 and Cm7-F7) originating from Dm7. At the beginning of this type of turnaround, the Dm7 will function as a "ii" chord and be paired with a G7 chord, creating a Dm7-G7 "ii-V" change. The G7 then creates a "V-i" cadence to the next chord, Cm7; then a "ii-V" change is executed from Cm7 (i.e., Cm7-F7) to bring us back to the tonic chord, B♭maj7 (the "I"). The end result is the following string of harmonic information: Dm7-G7-Cm7-F7-B♭maj7—and that's just the first two bars! The final two measures of this turnaround—B♭maj7 to F7—act as the "nail in the coffin," and contribute an even more convincing cadence, directing the band to return to the top of the tune.

Chromatically Descending Sequence of Dominant Seventh Chords

As an alternative to the "ii-V" chord cycle, consider a chromatically descending sequence of dominant seventh chords as a turnaround. In the key of B♭, after the tonic chord is stated (in this case, B♭7), shift the shape up a minor third (three frets) to D♭7, then backtrack in half steps until you return to B♭7.

From an accompaniment standpoint, this type of turnaround is a cakewalk. But from a soloist's perspective, nailing these changes can be trying. In the single-note example that accompanies the following turnaround, note the frequent use of chord tones (1-3-5-♭7) throughout the B♭7-D♭7-C7-C♭7 cycle. Needless to say, these tricky changes prove the importance of practicing arpeggios. Before you attempt your own improvisation over this chord sequence, make sure you "bone up" on all your dominant seventh chord arpeggio shapes—specifically B♭7 (B♭-D-F-A♭), D♭7 (D♭-F-A♭-C♭), C7 (C-E-G-B♭), and C♭7 (C♭-E♭-G♭-B♭♭) arpeggios.

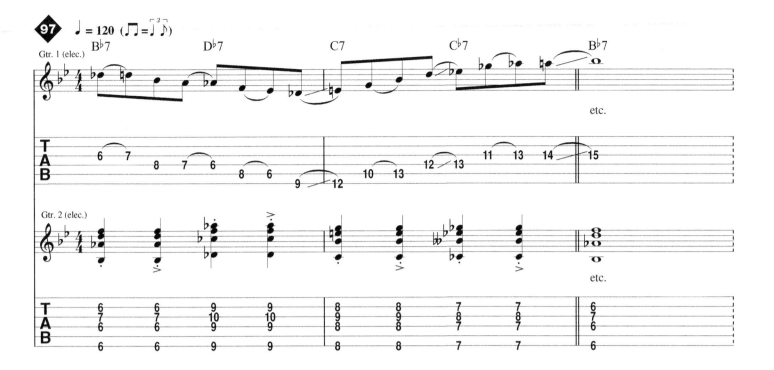

Major Seventh Chord Cycles

Another type of turnaround that relies on one chord type uses a string of major seventh chords to set up the return to the tune's tonic chord. In this next example, an Fmaj7 chord (the "I" chord) is stated, then another major seventh chord—in this case, A♭maj7—is inserted a minor third higher. From this point, a sequence reminiscent of a "ii-V-I" cycle takes over, though it's comprised strictly of major seventh chords: A♭maj7-D♭maj7-G♭maj7. Notice that this final chord, G♭maj7, sits one half step above your song's actual key (F)—a creative way to anticipate the chord at the top of the tune.

Before you try improvising through these changes, follow the same logic as in the previous example: polish up your major-seventh arpeggio chops. By honing in on the chord tones that comprise Fmaj7 (F-A-C-E), A♭maj7 (A♭-C-E♭-G), D♭maj7 (D♭-F-A♭-C), and G♭maj7 (G♭-B♭-D♭-F), you'll be ahead of the game when the time comes to "blow."

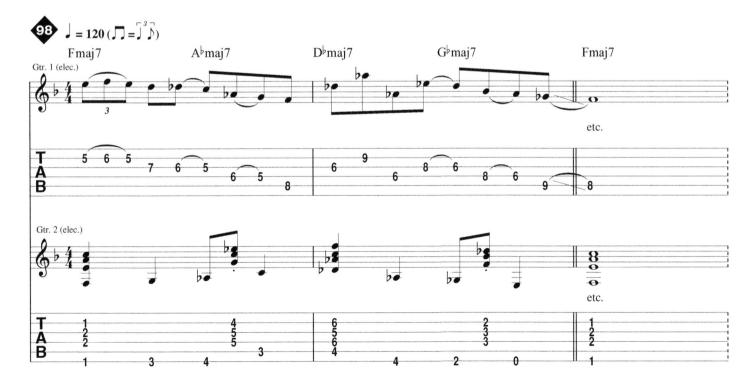

Minor Key Turnarounds [iim7♭5-V7alt-im9(maj7)]

In a jazz tune fixed in a minor tonality, the final four bars will most likely contain a hearty helping of altered dominant seventh chords, a "ii-V" cadence to a minor tonic chord (the "i")—even minor chords inflected with dissonant alterations/extensions like the major seventh and ninth.

In this final jazz turnaround, shown in the key of D minor, after a "♭VI" chord (B♭7) in the first bar, an A7(♯5) chord in measure 2 creates a "V-i" cadence to Dm9(maj7) in the third bar. The entire four-measure sequence is then punctuated with a minor "ii-V" change—in this case, Em7(♭5)–A7(♯5).

The sample lead line that accompanies this turnaround attacks the various chords in the following manner: B♭7(♯11)=B♭ Lydian Dominant (B♭-C-D-E-F-G-A♭); A7(♯5)=A Augmented (A-B♭-C♯-D♯-E-G); Dm9(maj7)=D Melodic Minor (D-E-F-G-A-B-C♯); Em7(♭5)=E Locrian (E-F-G-A-B♭-C-D); A7(♯5)=A Whole Tone fragment (C♯-D♯-E♯-G).

GUITAR NOTATION LEGEND

Guitar music can be notated three different ways: on a *musical staff*, in *tablature*, and in *rhythm slashes*.

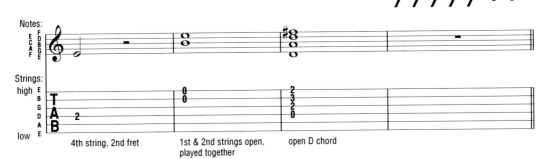

RHYTHM SLASHES are written above the staff. Strum chords in the rhythm indicated. Use the chord diagrams found at the top of the first page of the transcription for the appropriate chord voicings. Round noteheads indicate single notes.

THE MUSICAL STAFF shows pitches and rhythms and is divided by bar lines into measures. Pitches are named after the first seven letters of the alphabet.

TABLATURE graphically represents the guitar fingerboard. Each horizontal line represents a string, and each number represents a fret.

4th string, 2nd fret   1st & 2nd strings open, played together   open D chord

HALF-STEP BEND: Strike the note and bend up 1/2 step.

WHOLE-STEP BEND: Strike the note and bend up one step.

GRACE NOTE BEND: Strike the note and immediately bend up as indicated.

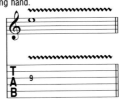

SLIGHT (MICROTONE) BEND: Strike the note and bend up 1/4 step.

BEND AND RELEASE: Strike the note and bend up as indicated, then release back to the original note. Only the first note is struck.

PRE-BEND: Bend the note as indicated, then strike it.

VIBRATO: The string is vibrated by rapidly bending and releasing the note with the fretting hand.

WIDE VIBRATO: The pitch is varied to a greater degree by vibrating with the fretting hand.

HAMMER-ON: Strike the first (lower) note with one finger, then sound the higher note (on the same string) with another finger by fretting it without picking.

PULL-OFF: Place both fingers on the notes to be sounded. Strike the first note and without picking, pull the finger off to sound the second (lower) note.

LEGATO SLIDE: Strike the first note and then slide the same fret-hand finger up or down to the second note. The second note is not struck.

SHIFT SLIDE: Same as legato slide, except the second note is struck.

TRILL: Very rapidly alternate between the notes indicated by continuously hammering on and pulling off.

TAPPING: Hammer ("tap") the fret indicated with the pick-hand index or middle finger and pull off to the note fretted by the fret hand.

NATURAL HARMONIC: Strike the note while the fret-hand lightly touches the string directly over the fret indicated.

PINCH HARMONIC: The note is fretted normally and a harmonic is produced by adding the edge of the thumb or the tip of the index finger of the pick hand to the normal pick attack.

PICK SCRAPE: The edge of the pick is rubbed down (or up) the string, producing a scratchy sound.

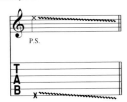

MUFFLED STRINGS: A percussive sound is produced by laying the fret hand across the string(s) without depressing, and striking them with the pick hand.

PALM MUTING: The note is partially muted by the pick hand lightly touching the string(s) just before the bridge.

RAKE: Drag the pick across the strings indicated with a single motion.

TREMOLO PICKING: The note is picked as rapidly and continuously as possible.

VIBRATO BAR DIVE AND RETURN: The pitch of the note or chord is dropped a specified number of steps (in rhythm), then returned to the original pitch.

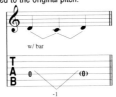

VIBRATO BAR SCOOP: Depress the bar just before striking the note, then quickly release the bar.

VIBRATO BAR DIP: Strike the note and then immediately drop a specified number of steps, then release back to the original pitch.

IMPROVE YOUR IMPROV

AND OTHER JAZZ TECHNIQUES WITH BOOKS FROM HAL LEONARD

JAZZ GUITAR

HAL LEONARD GUITAR METHOD
by Jeff Schroedl

The Hal Leonard Jazz Guitar Method is your complete guide to learning jazz guitar. This book uses real jazz songs to teach the basics of accompanying and improvising jazz guitar in the style of Wes Montgomery, Joe Pass, Tal Farlow, Charlie Christian, Pat Martino, Barney Kessel, Jim Hall, and many others.
00695359 Book/Online Audio $19.99

AMAZING PHRASING

50 WAYS TO IMPROVE YOUR
IMPROVISATIONAL SKILLS • *by Tom Kolb*

This book/CD pack explores all the main components necessary for crafting well-balanced rhythmic and melodic phrases. It also explains how these phrases are put together to form cohesive solos. Many styles are covered – rock, blues, jazz, fusion, country, Latin, funk and more – and all of the concepts are backed up with musical examples.
00695583 Book/CD Pack... $19.95

BEST OF JAZZ GUITAR

by Wolf Marshall • Signature Licks

In this book/CD pack, Wolf Marshall provides a hands-on analysis of 10 of the most frequently played tunes in the jazz genre, as played by the leading guitarists of all time. Each selection includes technical analysis and performance notes, biographical sketches, and authentic matching audio with backing tracks.
00695586 Book/CD Pack... $24.95

CHORD-MELODY PHRASES FOR GUITAR

by Ron Eschete • REH ProLessons Series

Expand your chord-melody chops with these outstanding jazz phrases! This book covers: chord substitutions, chromatic movements, contrary motion, pedal tones, inner-voice movements, reharmonization techniques, and much more. Includes standard notation and tab, and a CD.
00695628 Book/CD Pack... $17.99

CHORDS FOR JAZZ GUITAR

THE COMPLETE GUIDE TO COMPING,
CHORD MELODY AND CHORD SOLOING • *by Charlton Johnson*

This book/CD pack will teach you how to play jazz chords all over the fretboard in a variety of styles and progressions. It covers: voicings, progressions, jazz chord theory, comping, chord melody, chord soloing, voice leading and many more topics. The CD includes 98 full-band demo tracks. No tablature.
00695706 Book/CD Pack... $19.95

FRETBOARD ROADMAPS – JAZZ GUITAR

THE ESSENTIAL GUITAR PATTERNS
THAT ALL THE PROS KNOW AND USE • *by Fred Sokolow*

This book/CD pack will get guitarists playing lead & rhythm anywhere on the fretboard, in any key! It teaches a variety of lead guitar styles using moveable patterns, double-note licks, sliding pentatonics and more, through easy-to-follow diagrams and instructions. The CD includes 54 full-demo tracks.
00695354 Book/CD Pack... $14.95

JAZZ IMPROVISATION FOR GUITAR

by Les Wise • REH ProLessons Series

This book/CD will allow you to make the transition from playing disjointed scales and arpeggios to playing melodic jazz solos that maintain continuity and interest for the listener. Topics covered include: tension and resolution, major scale, melodic minor scale, and harmonic minor scale patterns, common licks and substitution techniques, creating altered tension, and more! Features standard notation and tab, and a CD.
00695657 Book/CD Pack... $16.95

JAZZ RHYTHM GUITAR

THE COMPLETE GUIDE
by Jack Grassel

This book/CD pack will help rhythm guitarists better understand: chord symbols and voicings, comping styles and patterns, equipment, accessories and set-up, the fingerboard, chord theory, and much more. The accompanying CD includes 74 full-band tracks.
00695654 Book/CD Pack... $19.95

JAZZ SOLOS FOR GUITAR

LEAD GUITAR IN THE STYLES OF TAL FARLOW,
BARNEY KESSEL, WES MONTGOMERY, JOE PASS, JOHNNY SMITH
by Les Wise

Examine the solo concepts of the masters with this book including phrase-by-phrase performance notes, tips on arpeggio substitution, scale substitution, tension and resolution, jazz-blues, chord soloing, and more. The CD includes full demonstration and rhythm-only tracks.
00695447 Book/CD Pack... $17.95

100 JAZZ LESSONS

Guitar Lesson Goldmine Series
by John Heussenstamm and Paul Silbergleit

Featuring 100 individual modules covering a giant array of topics, each lesson includes detailed instruction with playing examples presented in standard notation and tablature. You'll also get extremely useful tips, scale diagrams, and more to reinforce your learning experience, plus 2 full audio CDs featuring performance demos of all the examples in the book!
00696454 Book/2-CD Pack $24.99

101 MUST-KNOW JAZZ LICKS

A QUICK, EASY REFERENCE GUIDE
FOR ALL GUITARISTS • *by Wolf Marshall*

Here are 101 definitive licks, plus demonstration audio, from every major jazz guitar style, neatly organized into easy-to-use categories. They're all here: swing and pre-bop, bebop, post-bop modern jazz, hard bop and cool jazz, modal jazz, soul jazz and postmodern jazz. Includes an introduction, tips, and a list of suggested recordings.
00695433 Book/Online Audio $17.99

SWING AND BIG BAND GUITAR

FOUR-TO-THE-BAR COMPING IN THE STYLE OF
FREDDIE GREEN • *by Charlton Johnson*

This unique package teaches the essentials of swing and big band styles, including chord voicings, inversions, substitutions; time and groove, reading charts, chord reduction, and expansion; sample songs, patterns, progressions, and exercises; chord reference library; and a CD with over 50 full-demo examples. Uses chord grids – no tablature.
00695147 Book/CD Pack... $19.99

FOR MORE INFORMATION, SEE YOUR LOCAL MUSIC DEALER,
OR WRITE TO:

HAL•LEONARD®
CORPORATION
7777 W. BLUEMOUND RD. P.O. BOX 13819 MILWAUKEE, WI 53213

Visit Hal Leonard Online at **www.halleonard.com**

Prices, contents and availability subject to change without notice.

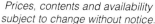

0416